GW01401196

WISDOM AND WIT

AN ANTHOLOGY FROM THE WRITINGS OF GORDON RUPP

Compiled and edited by
John A. Vickers

Wisdom and Wit
An anthology from the writings of Gordon Rupp
© Introduction John A. Vickers

We are grateful to the *Methodist Recorder* for the use of the photographs on the front cover and page 6 which are their copyright.

Published on behalf of World Methodist Historical Society
by Methodist Publishing House, 20 Ivatt Way, Peterborough PE3 7PG

ISBN 1 85852 003 7

INTRODUCTION

Gordon Rupp's standing as either historian or communicator needs no bush. He was a prolific and versatile writer, and this anthology is drawn from a variety of sources, ranging from his journalistic contributions in the *Manchester Guardian* and the *Methodist Recorder* to a handful of large-scale works, from broadcast talks printed in *The Listener* to academic papers in learned journals.

His field was equally wide, with the Protestant Reformation and the Evangelical Revival as its focal points. Though deeply rooted in this Protestant soil, his ecclesiastical sympathies were as eclectic as his literary taste. His writing bears manifold witness to the assertion 'that the truth is diverse and many-sided, that catholicity demands not uniformity but variety' – a view which, he once said, 'would have seemed to most 16th and 17th century Christians like the apostolic nightmare in which St. Peter beheld a sheet full of all manner of creeping things'. He used to tell his Catholic students, 'We shall get along very well if you remember that I mean by "Protestant" roughly what you mean by "Catholic".'

Unlike some of his younger contemporaries, he was well versed in the theological dimension of the church's history. On the other hand, he was ill at ease with the more recent sociological and statistical approaches, a limitation that surfaced in his last major work, *Religion in England 1688-1791*, as reviewers were not slow to point out. The obverse of this, for the general reader in particular, was his ability to visualize and bring to life both characters and situations from the past with an immediacy not often found in academic writing.

His extensive and varied reading is clearly reflected, as he moves, sure-footed and light-fingered, through the world's literature. Dante and Milton, Watts and (of course) Charles Wesley are here by divine right. So, too, is Bunyan who, as a man of the people, had a special niche in his affections. In lighter vein, Chesterton, W. S. Gilbert, Lewis Carroll and Wodehouse emerge as clear favourites – though surprisingly, perhaps, he does not seem to have been drawn to Jerome K. Jerome, Saki or more recent humorists like Ogden Nash.

Like Martin Luther, he was one of those 'who delight not only by what they say, but by the way they say it'. He appreciated Luther's 'elephantine' sense of humour, commenting wryly that 'since it was often misunderstood by his contemporaries, it can be imagined what a mine of potential misconception it bequeathed to owl-like theologians fumbling with what is called "the jocular element in Luther".' That something of the London *gamin* lived on in the distinguished academic is amply illustrated in the following pages. In his own words, written of his fellow Londoner Sir Thomas More, he had 'that dead pan quality of humour which is as recognizable and distinct as that of a Brooklyn taxi-driver'.

Chesterton's common sense and sense of humour were a decisive influence in his mid-teens as he found his way back from unbelief to a reasoned faith. 'For me, too, humour was something important and to be taken seriously,' he wrote many years later, adding in another place, 'and of such, if the parables of Jesus are anything to go by, is the Kingdom of Heaven'. (Such, indeed, was his devotion to G.K.C. that he more than once credited him with Sidney Smith's quip about the two housewives arguing from opposite premises.) This was the man who, as Public Orator, could present the Chief Constable of Manchester for an honorary degree with the words, 'It's a fair cop'![1] To criticism of his flippancy his unrepentant response was that wits were in much shorter supply than half-wits.

Rupp's thinking was often concrete and pictorial, to the immeasurable benefit of his readers, as when he writes: 'The world of the New Testament is a world of great heights and depths, of horrifying, dangerous abysses, and wonderful, breathtaking views, precipices and summits. I wonder whether Christians have not too often turned it into a kind of seaside resort, a smooth and rounded mediocrity, a life-style with no cutting edge, nothing much to distinguish us from our pagan neighbours . . . a religion 500,000 miles wide and half an inch deep.'

As this passage reminds us, for all his flippancy the serious side of Gordon Rupp is not in doubt. The fateful year 1936-7 found him engrossed in post-graduate studies at Strasbourg and Basle, in the course of which he became fluent in German and made lasting friendships. These were the advantages that caught the attention of Bishop George Bell, who took him on his visit to the German Churches in the immediate aftermath of the War. Rupp's memories of that visit – the devastation and harrowing conditions, and above all the deeply

---

[1]   I owe this reference to a 'pen portrait' by Marcus Ward in the *Methodist Recorder*, 13 June 1968.

moving encounter with German Evangelical church leaders in Stuttgart – were vividly recalled in later years and influenced him profoundly.

Here was one academic who was able to appreciate the qualities needed by men of action, while recognizing that 'to be able to keep an open mind required detachment from the hurly-burly of decision, and is more easily achieved in academic groves than in the battlefield or market-place or temple.'

He saw history in terms not so much of mountain peaks as of a coral reef, formed by countless minor deposits.[2] So he delighted to exalt the 'common man' – and woman – and to focus down from the generalizations and abstractions of academic history to the level of personal and domestic reality: Luther's wife struggling with her husband's open-handed generosity, Carlstadt's young wife worn out by endlessly traipsing the roads of Europe, the theological students in Martin Bucer's household entrusted with the pleasurable task of catechizing the maid-servants . . .

The material and spiritual realms were never far removed from each other in his mind. While examining the Lectures on Romans as evidence of Luther's theological development, he also enables us to picture them being delivered 'as the days and months rolled on, from the dim, chilly hours of winter to the warm, drenching sunshine of the summer, to an audience which, like all academic audiences in all times and places, rendered attention fitfully, always eager to be distracted by a gust of wind or a vagrant butterfly'. As in the gospel parables, he illuminates the divine/human relationship by comparing it with everyday human ones: 'When two people are in love, and sure of each other . . . they do not reckon up the size of their gifts to one another, or how expensive they are . . . This fact, that faith does away with quantitative measurement of services, is a profound comment on the nature of the Christian religion, and cuts deep into the heart of the practical abuses of the late medieval Church.'

He had an enviable gift for finding, and interpreting, the significant details in great works of art, with Breughel as a predictable favourite. Part and parcel with this, the most mundane and everyday observation –

---

2   All the same, he recognized that 'in comparison with the great pressures of history, even the giants are but dwarfs.' ('Luther and the Reformation', in *The Reformation Crisis*, 1965, p.30)

grafitti on a Cambridge wall, love letters ('only ink marks on paper', but sacramental in their significance), football supporters on the terraces – became meaningful for him, and therefore to his hearers or readers. He is almost the only outstanding academic I can envisage being entirely at home in a fish-and-chip queue.

The compilation of this anthology has proved to be a proleptic fulfilment of a suggestion made in the somewhat belated obituary in the *Proceedings of the British Academy*[3] – that 'a book of the wit and wisdom of Gordon Rupp could make compelling reading'. The anthology was already at proof stage when this appeared and I have deviated from it only to the extent of giving priority to his wisdom in my title.

Others knew Gordon Rupp far longer and more intimately than I can claim to have done, and therefore had the better claim to prepare this anthology had they chosen. Their lost opportunity has been my gain. Reading through almost every word he ever published has been a labour of love indeed. My task has been that of emulating Little Jack Horner, of putting in my thumb and pulling out plums.[4] If the result does less than justice to the whole pie, it may at least serve to whet the appetite for more; and the reader will not be disappointed.

I cherish the memory of our association in his closing years and of his encouragement and support for my editorial work on the fourth volume of the *History of the Methodist Church in Great Britain*, in which he took an unfailing (if often illegible) interest. My last memory of him typifies the man who loved to represent the Church as servant, the Bride of Christ disguised as Cinderella. At the end of a group visit to Cambridge my wife and I found the Dixie Professor of Ecclesiastical History in the church kitchen, unostentatiously getting down to the washing up while everyone else was touring the premises. This has been my yardstick for greatness in the Kingdom of Heaven ever since.

John A. Vickers

3   Vol.80 (1993), pp.493-8
4   In a Christmas sermon, Rupp himself could not refrain from a reference to 'sermons in plum stones' – not one of his most apposite allusions!

EDITORIAL NOTE

After a short selection of *hors d'oeuvres* the extracts are arranged chronologically rather than by topic, to foster serendipity. But a short subject index will be found at the end for those prepared to cheat.

A number of friends have helped me trace some of the more elusive lectures and articles, notably Mr E. Alan Rose and the late Elizabeth Hart. I am indebted to them and to all those who replied to my appeal for reminiscences of Gordon Rupp. All but two of the publishers approached readily gave their permission for extracts to be reprinted.

In particular, the anthology would not have been possible without the interest and approval of Mr Martin Rupp.

The publication of this anthology will benefit the E. Gordon Rupp Memorial Fund, set up in 1988 to provide bursaries for younger scholars in the field of Reformation studies. Contributions to the Fund may be sent to the Treasurer at Wesley House, Jesus Lane, Cambridge CB5 8BJ.

ACKNOWLEDGMENTS

Permission to reprint has been granted by the following publishers: Allen & Unwin; Cambridge University Press; T & T Clark; Epworth Press; Lutterworth Press; Oxford University Press; SCM Press; Scolar Press; Sheldon Press and Sylvan Press; and by the publishers and editors of the periodicals and newspapers cited in the text. To all of these we express our gratitude.

President of Conference

APPETIZERS

To all study of past theology the important thing is to allow for and discover the angle of refraction. (1945)

You do not get dry rot out of a house by giving it another coat of paint. (1946)

The recording of acknowledgments is one of the devices by which the undistinguished compound for their own obscurity by making more reputable scholars go bail on their behalf. (1947)

Evangelical Arminianism stands for the historical point where we came in – for Christian doctrine, as with old wine, the date is as important as the label. (1949)

History is the lynch law of the universe, rough justice, perverted by the perversity of sin, but still a witness to our human solidarity and the moral law. (1949)

God's commands [for the Christian are not] like the regulations of a factory, of a barracks, or even the laws of cricket; they are the good manners of the home life of the children of God . . . not regulations, but the unfolding implications of God's promise and gift to us in Jesus Christ. (1949)

. . . the catholic spirit of love without which the ecumenical movement would become the last desperate gamble of Ecclesiastical Man to regain power in the modern world. (1950)

Nothing shows up the real character of tyranny than when, stripped of glamour and romanticism, it is shown doing mean and shabby things to little people. (1953)

Some words may be likened to a single note in music: they have one clear and distinct definition. It was one of the merits of scholasticism that it had achieved a technical vocabulary of such precision. But there are other words which are more like chords of music, rich complexities. Many of the great Biblical notions are of this kind. (1953)

Perhaps it was the tragedy of Methodism that it produced in Jabez Bunting a great statesman when above all things it most needed a prophet. (1953)

7

So many princes and potentates came to have a vested interest in Erasmus that he almost resembled the Duke of Plaza Toro who turned himself into a limited liability company. (1953)

Ecumenical English is the new industrial disease.[5] (1954)

College tutors, it is well known, were instituted in the time of man's innocence, for the procreation of spiritual children, and also for the mutual help and comfort that the one ought to have for the other. (1954)

The art of sitting on half a dozen fences at once was little cultivated in nineteenth-century Methodism. (1954)

The cheapest of all the gifts of the Holy Ghost is the gift of the gab. (1954)

[The American team at the World Methodist Conference] is noticeably lacking in spin bowlers. (1955)

Methodists . . . pride themselves on the brotherhood of their ministry, and . . . have no leaders they cannot pick up and spank and put down, as on occasion the Conference from time to time is pleased to do. (1956)

. . . the complacent assumptions of a literary world which seems a little crowded with the descendants of lapsed Dissenters. (1957)

Macaulay's Puritan turns out, often, to be a Clapham evangelical in fancy dress. (1957)

To describe Cranmer's Litany as a lovely service would indeed be rather like describing the Day of Judgment as a pretty sight. (1957)

The Protestantism of Kingsley's *Westward Ho!* is a kind of Pre-Raphaelite view of Elizabeth's day. (1957)

In these days a virile Roman Church is less aptly symbolized by Bunyan's gibbering, toothless, senile Giant Pope than by some stalwart tough (with padded shoulders!) playing football for Notre Dame. (1957)

---

5   A neat deflection of Philip Guedalla's assertion that 'Historian's English is not a style; it is an industrial disease.'

. . . the sanctified smirk . . . which appears on the lips of most ministers who dandle an infant at the font. (1958)

[The language of Tillich's *Systematic Theology*] . . . a pre-fabricated theological jargon invented by the author, of almost unimaginable inelegance, a compound of refugee English and theologian's American. (1958)

For some years now it has been my regular penitential discipline to read side by side the correspondence columns of the *Church Times* and of the *Methodist Recorder*. (1958)

If every speaker, beforehand, would really pray Psalm 39:1-4, then perhaps more audiences might not feel that for them the most appropriate litany would be the prayers for those at sea. (1962)

Martin Luther is in relation to the Reformation rather like the opening notes of some great piano concerto – say Beethoven's Fourth – which states the theme, which is then taken up by other instruments and finally lost in the developing pattern of the music. (1965)

Christian schools are not ideological betting shops rigged always to come out on the side of the ecclesiastical bookies. (1965)

The normative word about Christian renewal is not 'revival' but 'resurrection'. (1965)

The 'Order for the Day' of Martin Bucer's household in Cambridge laid down that the two theological student boarders were to catechize the maids, and we may guess it was the most pleasant of their household duties. (1967)

. . . the beauty of our English language, that daily sacrifice offered and mutilated on the altar of the Ecumenical Movement. (1967)

I have some sympathy nowadays for the conservative temper. It is the 'liturgical gnats' rather than the 'theological camels' which are the hardest to swallow. (1970)

Righteous indignation has always been a dangerous luxury for religious men. (1972)

9

If British Methodism had a coat of arms a cup of tea rampant would certainly have to appear on it. (1974)

In the end the difficult thing about the Christian religion is not its intricacy, but its simplicity: not what we find hard to understand, but what confronts our souls directly with choice and action. (1978)

John Wesley turned to Augustine for a doctrine of prevenient grace which marks off his Arminianism from the dehydrated, semi-Pelagianism of the Anglican Establishment. (1985)

. . . that most insidious of all radicalisms, innovation based on an appeal to tradition, to a past that never was. (1986)

WISDOM AND WIT

1941

When a great word is cheapened it becomes a positive danger. What is a battle-cry in one generation may become a catchword in the next. In ancient Israel the prophet Isaiah fanned the hopes of his people to a Great Deliverance by the thought of the sacred temple. But by the time of Jeremiah and Ezekiel the great phrase, 'The Temple of the Lord!' had become a glib expression which hid the reality of national apostasy and lured it to disaster. And what is a catchword in the second generation may become a by-word and a jest in the third. And this is most perilous of all.
(*Is this a Christian Country?* p.3)

We assume too easily that our national ideals are Christian because they seem to us to be fine and splendid and right. We need to prove them at the bar of Faith, for it has been well said that not only men, but their ideas must repent before the Cross.
(Ibid, p.9)

Protestants have been too fond of regarding themselves as called after the order of Melchizedek, 'without father, without mother, without descent'. But Christians may not 'contract out' of their past even when it seems disagreeable or even shameful to them . . . When all is said and done, the Reformers owed more to the medieval Church than to the Bogomiles, the Waldenses, the Cathari, the Spiritual Franciscans or even the Lollards and the followers of Huss.
(Ibid, pp.11-12)

Much nonsense has been written about the 'Priesthood of all Believers'. It has even, with an inverted sacerdotalism, been treated as though it meant the 'Laity of All the Priesthood' and that ministers and laymen are all equal, especially the laymen.
(Ibid, pp.26-7; cf *The Righteousness of God* (1953), p.315)

Despite Lecky, it was Puritanism rather than Methodism which saved us from a French Revolution, for the decisive influences were exerted before 1688.
(Ibid, pp.28-9)

11

John Wesley did not aim to raise a troop of pale young curates, profound, distinguished and unintelligible: his Helpers, a few parsons, tradesmen and ex-soldiers, were more like a gang of highwaymen, conspiring together to round England, calling the miners of Wales and Cornwall, the workers of the North, the soldiers of the Flemish camps, to stand and deliver to the Word.
(Ibid, p.45)

If the thought of national judgment is hard, there is an even harder suggestion by St John in the Apocalypse. For of the Heavenly City it is written that 'the nations shall walk in the light thereof'. Can we think of a nation being taken into heaven? Is it not crude to suggest that the New Jerusalem is like modern Rome, with an English colony about the Spanish steps and an Olde English Tea Shoppe with stale buns and tepid tea? Yet all our thinking about what eye has not seen is bound to be done in pictures, and can at best be in the form of a creative myth. If we shut our eyes and screw them tight we may try to imagine Dr Inge's 'Kingdom of Absolute Values', but we shall probably not be much wiser . . .
(Ibid, p.57)

It isn't enough to give a label to an idea. The important thing is not, 'Where does it come from?' but 'Is it true?' A hungry man asks of a plate of food, 'Can I eat it?', not 'Who cooked it?' Yet the question of origin may be important. A man's appetite might vanish if he found he was lunching with the Borgias.
(Ibid, p.62)

1942

[Bilney] denied some of the articles laid against him and said that others were garbled misquotations from the sermons he had preached in Norwich and London. This is highly probable, and there can be few preachers who would care to stand their trial on what their congregations remember of their sermons.
('The "Recantation" of Thomas Bilney', in *London Quarterly and Holborn Review, 1942*, p.181)

* * *

[Luther's] enemies have not been more agreed about him than his friends, and the sharp etchings of the radical Protestants have little more in common with the Catholic cartoons than the melancholy consensus that Martin Luther, though Lamentably Memorable, was a Bad Thing. ('Luther – the Catholic Caricature', in *Theology*, October 1942, p.198)

Antipathy sees clearer than the purblind devotion which shatters truth to bits and then remoulds it nearer to the heart's desire. If for no other reason than this, no student can afford to ignore the Catholic caricature which was the counterpart of the Protestant 'Luther legend'. (Ibid, p.199)

M. Maritain's brilliant essay on 'Luther: ou l'avenement du moi', in his *Trois Reformateurs* (1925) is a horrid example of what can happen when Clio gets into the hands of the philosophers. In this kind of essay, with which our time abounds, history is used much as the preacher uses sermon illustrations: the facts have to fit a preconceived pattern of generalizations, in this case the theme 'metaphysical egocentrism'. Anybody with time and ingenuity could make an equally good and equally one-sided illustration of Erasmus, or Ignatius Loyola, since only a selection of the facts is necessary. (Ibid, p.202)

1945

Mr Weiner's book[6] is the *reductio ad absurdum* of modern tendencies in the writing of history: the subjectivism which would reduce everything to 'anyhow in my interpretation'; the scorn for 'scientific history'; the overworking of the Crocean half truth that all history is contemporary. Behind Mr Weiner stands M. Funck Brentano, whose poet's eye in a fine frenzy rolling abandons accuracy for brightness of style, and M. Maritain, whose treatment of Luther in *Three Reformers* shows how slovenly and shoddy a great philosopher can become when he gets off his subject. (*Martin Luther – Hitler's Cause – or Cure?* p.6)

---

6   *Martin Luther: Hitler's Spiritual Ancestor.* Rupp had earlier drawn attention to the fact that even someone as eminent and well informed as William Temple could put forward the view that 'Luther prepared the way for Hitler'. (*Theology*, October 1942, p.204)

13

We have already quoted the appeal to Luther made in the Norwegian protest against Jewish persecution. 'Luther said . . .': if these be illustrations of what the Dean of St Paul's has called that 'tiresome deference to the authority of Luther which seems so inexplicable to an Anglican', one can only say that comparisons are odious, but that a little more deference to some kind of prophetic authority might have enabled the Church of England to bear a little more of its share of the charges of the 'Crown Rights of the Redeemer' in the last three centuries.
(Ibid, p.68)

* * *

In the autumn of 1945 Rupp accompanied Bishop Bell on a visit to post-war Germany, where they witnessed the wholesale urban destruction, the total disruption of normal life and the early efforts of the allied armies to deal with the problems of food shortages, disease and disrupted communications. (Their meeting at Stuttgart with leaders of the German Evangelical Church is described elsewhere.)

I had a long talk with Dr Melle, President of the German Methodist Church (whose unfortunate utterances here in 1937 are still remembered). He expressed sincere regret and, I think, real repentance for the past. But one cannot feel very thrilled by the record of German Methodism under Hitler, or even cheered by the fact that at present Methodism in Germany is meeting no more hindrance from the Russians than it had from the Nazis . . . At lunch it transpired that Dr Melle had kept unimpaired the witness for non-smoking and total abstinence, while his partner at table, Pastor Grueber, confessed that, for his part, he, a total abstainer and Good Templar, had broken the pledge in the concentration camp which the Methodists had avoided. It seems that even non-smokers and total abstainers may miss the meaning of Christian citizenship.
('In Darkest Germany: Condition of the Churches', *Methodist Recorder*, 15 November 1945)

1946

I do not know who has done most harm, historians who know no theology or the theologians who are careless of that historical context without which theology is but half explained . . .

Those who sigh after some alternative reformation 'from within' which might have been but for Luther can hardly have considered the long centuries during which 'reform of the church in head and members' had lain unsettled on a thousand clerical agendas . . . It is customary to describe this wholly imaginary alternative as being 'along Erasmian lines'. I fear these Erasmian lines mask an illusion as dangerous as the famous lines of Maginot. I seem to see four hundred years of European intellectuals entrenched behind these lines, beautiful and ineffectual angels who have never considered the gravity of sin, themselves very neatly by-passed by forces of human evil which have compassed us all with the threat of ruin, and for which they cannot escape a measure of responsibility.
('Martin Luther, 1546-1946: A Free Church Commemoration', in *London Quarterly and Holborn Review*, 1946, p. 108)

There are large areas of Europe where Protestantism has been grievously, perhaps mortally wounded. What have we said about it? Dare we pay homage to the great rebel and applaud his daring, and go contentedly away, smug with the passing of some resolution or, with even greater boldness, the sending of a deputation to the Prime Minister? Have we even considered risking our reputation (already a little damaged) by solemnly rebuking our nation and our government? Must we always limp behind the pacifists and the left-wing intellectuals and plead in the name of humanity and never, never speak to our people of what they must say and do simply for the sake of our Lord Jesus Christ? I cannot thank God for Martin Luther without remembering Martin Niemoller who was howled down by German students last week for taking such a risk and making such a gesture for the sake of Christians everywhere, and I cannot remember either without knowing that they both, Martin Luther and Martin Niemoller, were Germans and my brothers in Christ. At least, must we not affirm our solidity with them and reaffirm our solemn responsibility as Free Churchmen for Protestantism in Europe?
(Ibid, pp.112-13)

1947

John Frith was the prodigy among [the Cambridge reformers], and won such pity from his captors that they would have connived at his escape. 'If I should now start and run away, I should run away from my God,' was the reply. It took courage, at 24, to set one's face steadfastly towards Smithfield, and he died in 1533 upon articles so mildly heretical that he may almost be said to have died to make the Church safe for the Oxford Movement.

(University Sermon on 'The Cambridge Reformers', printed in *The Cambridge Review*, January 25, 1947)

There are strains and stresses in all our human existence, pressures under which the kaleidoscopic patterns of the different centuries resolve into primary elements, things hoped, feared, suffered by all men, making us all contemporary with one another. 'From plague, pestilence and famine: from battle, murder and sudden death, Good Lord deliver us.' Cranmer's Litany speaks for countless men and women in the last ten years in moments when, the smooth and rounded mediocrity of civilized life shattered, they have felt alone and afraid at the mercy of the universe, and so on the very edge of the discovery that it is God who has us all at his mercy, and precisely there.

(Ibid)

The Reformation involved the interruption of the intellectual work of the Renaissance. True, our age ought to know better than most that one generation must sometimes pay the cost of centuries of tranquil apostasy, that there are some calls for which other things must be set aside, or left to those who follow after. Civil war in Christendom left the Church obsessed with problems of its own existence. There went apart from it into the modern world a tradition of truth, in letters, in science and in philosophy, to shape some of the most splendid achievements, and some of the deadliest intellectual heresies of the modern age. There went out a tradition of justice which was to germinate the operative idealisms, the revolutionary dynamisms of the last three centuries. To them, even in their most arrogant and anti-clerical distortions, the Church, by reason of its own sin, cannot return an unqualified denial. It is clear that the reconciliation of the lost traditions of humanism and liberalism can never be achieved by a Church backward looking because inwardly afraid, meeting a new world with bitter truculence. But the failure is not only on the intellectual level. That the dark evils of our time should centre in Germany, home of the Reformation, and in Italy, heart of the Counter-Reformation, that the two Anglo-Saxon nations should inaugurate atomic warfare, is a comment, not only on what Hooker called 'the foggy damp of original corruption', but on four centuries of lost Christian opportunities. The call to penitence which comes from the 'Church under the Cross' in Germany is a reminder to Christendom that God might deal more easily with a desperate world than with an unrepentant Church.

Yet, with all their fine insight, won through heroic suffering, it seems that our Christian brethren on the Continent stand, with the rest of us, on the wrong side of the gulf which separates all Christendom from the common life of modern man. If our Gospel is to come home to an estranged humanity, it may be that the works of the Reformation must be done again, that there must be such a ferment within the Church as will produce new vocabularies, new forms of worship, new institutions, forms of Christian existence as different from those we have known as our own differ from those of the Middle Ages. Such changes are not to be enterprised from an unclean itch for innovation, by those who lay irreverent, ignorant or careless hands upon an historic inheritance. They demand a Church sensitive and obedient to the creative monitions of the Holy Ghost.
(Ibid)

* * *

The English Reformation is not wholly to be explained in terms of that conspiracy by which a lustful monarchy and predatory gentry combined to plunder the Church and rend the unity of Christendom. It had, after all, something to do with the beliefs of Christian men, and that not only in the breaking of an old order, but in the making of the new.
(*Studies in the Making of the English Protestant Tradition*, p.xi)

The spirit of individualist secularism did not originate in the sinister Protestant setting of sixteenth-century Germany, England or Holland, but in Italy, in the heart of Catholic Christendom where it had never died, though perhaps it had slumbered, since the ancient world. The Church of Santa Croce in Florence is the Westminster Abbey of modern man. Who views there the monuments which that city has raised to its children, Dante, Michelangelo, Leonardo, Bruni, Galileo, Machiavelli, cannot doubt where lies the watershed between medieval and modern Europe, and in all essentials the secular spirit will be found in the cities and states of medieval Italy. Thomas Cromwell, hobnobbing with Italian prelates, princes and merchant bankers, was meeting men no better and no worse than several generations of their fathers whose portraits fill the art galleries of the world, and which can be labelled 'Portrait of a hard-faced Business Man'. The hands are those of the Courtier of Castiglione, but the eyes and mouth belong to Samuel Smiles.
(Ibid, pp.xii-xiii)

Those who in our time speak smoothly of the benefits of persecution, of its power to stimulate flagging energies, and to weed the faint-hearted, would find little encouragement in the real story of the Church suffering here on earth. It is the fact that persecution has often been terribly successful. It is the fact that, even where it has failed, it has left its own peculiar legacy of spiritual diseases. How many ills of the fourth-century church are due, not to that much-abused conversion of Constantine, but to the tangled legacy of the preceding persecutions? Who, looking at French Protestantism with sympathy, cannot but feel that it has been cheated of its contribution to the religious life of Europe by the effect of the persecutions it has undergone? It is the fact that to live through a time of persecution – the Church under the Cross in modern Europe attests it beyond dispute – means to undergo strains and stresses which take grievous toll of spiritual and moral energies.
(Ibid, p.195)

* * *

There is a certain consecrated cussedness in the Puritan temper which has brought us too many liberties to be despised, least of all in 1947, and it is as well to remember that while it may be entreated, no power on earth can drive it.
('The Holy Communion in the Methodist Church', in *The Holy Communion: a Symposium,* p.121)

For the Methodist preacher the Holy Communion is in some sort the climax of his pastoral care . . . It is his intention to do what the Lord of the Church does, to break the Bread of Life to pardoned sinners. As he sees each little company, kneeling, with outstretched hands, the saints whose shoes he is not worthy to unloose, the difficult ones for whom the Church must always be something of a hospital, the little ones who must not be made to stumble, and those, unknown to him, but known to God, whom deep need has constrained, an assurance is given him that the Lord is truly present, pardoning, healing, offering through his own bloody Sacrifice that which is all our hope and which is alone our peace.

For the Methodist 'wonder' is an even greater word than 'mystery', and Holy Communion is, above all, the sacrament of wonder. Here, with his brethren he adores the Trinity in Unity, and bows subdued by
> The speechless awe that dares not move
> And all the silent heaven of love.
(Ibid, pp.125-6)

If we possessed only the solo part of a great concerto, there would be much to be learned from it of the beauty and genius of the whole work; and yet, because we lacked the orchestral setting and missed the musical conversation between solo and orchestra, we should misunderstand much of its meaning. We could call in the experts, and they would help us by interpreting the details, and by comparing the work with others by the same composer, or with the music of the period, but in the end they too would have to guess. It is a little like that with the letter to the Colossians. We have this brilliant solo by St Paul, but important features of the conversation of which it was the dominant part escape us.
(*The King of Glory: Studies in St Paul's Epistle to the Colossians*, p.3)

Paradoxically enough the importance of Colossae lies in its comparative unimportance, in the fact that it was 'without doubt . . . the least important church to which any epistle of St Paul was addressed' (Lightfoot). This was the Little Puddlecombe of the Apostolic Age, the ecclesiastical equivalent of the 'little man'.
(Ibid, p.5)

Those who sell flashy, ready-made mental suits at cut prices have always a certain plausibility. One reason why fancy religions flourish in garden suburbs and at seaside resorts is that they flatter those who are comfortable enough to dabble in religion, and educated enough to be susceptible to mental snobbery, but not alert enough to discriminate between new truth and ancient error. Christian Science, Spiritualism and Theosophy all offer as new truths a series of antiquated fallacies which go back through ancient Gnosticism to the pre-Christian world.
(Ibid, pp.8-9)

The Christian gospel is not one more remedy, to take its place along the row of medicine bottles on the shelf of a desperately sick humanity. Nor is it concerned only with that bit of life which interests religious people. Every glimpse of truth, beauty and goodness, all natural science, artistic creation, political experiment, have some relation to [Christ's] purposes. The man who sets off on some lonely adventure after truth, at all costs, and for its own sake, may depart from the crowd knowing that if he is faithful, every step will take him nearer the truth as it is in Jesus Christ, the Author of all truth and spiritual integrity. Nor is the gospel the peculiar and private property of a sect called Christians; for Christ is the King and Head of the whole human race, and through

him the entire universe may return to its true direction and find its peace and order and joy . . . There is nothing in the vast cosmos which is left outside the scope of God's creative and redeeming purposes which in Christ have become one (Col.1:20).
(Ibid, pp.14-15)

1949

At the beginning of the Victorian era, the dominant political tradition among the Methodists was Christian Toryism. Jabez Bunting was its redoubtable exponent. It would be superficial to write this off as mere reactionary fear of revolution or an other-worldly pietism. The enemies of Bunting complained that his politics were too definite, not that he had none, and they mocked him for haunting the House of Commons, pockets stuffed wide with newspapers and Parliamentary Reports, when he might have been reading his Bible. Bunting represents a classic Christian tradition of Christian Obedience, the tradition of the Duties as against the Rights of Man, the tradition from which Edmund Burke and John Wesley had impeached the revolutionary and rationalist idealism of Priestley and of Price. In protesting against the swelling Liberalism, Bunting anticipated the Oxford Movement and the Papal Syllabus of 1864, though he would hardly thank us for putting him in such Popish company. The result was that a European-wide tension met inside Methodism in a grievous domestic conflict which cost it one hundred thousand members in a few months. But when the disciplinary counter attack of the Methodist Conference was denounced by all other Nonconformists, and the indignation of British opinion was voiced by *The Times*, it was in a letter to that journal (which they would not print) that a Methodist preacher upheld the 'Crown Rights of the Redeemer' as surely as any John Knox or Hildebrand. 'You forget,' he said, 'that we are a religious and not a secular society. We guard against those terms and usages which would assimilate us to the House of Commons or any other secular assembly.' Modern Christians have not always understood as well how to protest against that most subtle of all despotisms, the tyranny of an operative and national idealism, or to resist the most insidious of all temptations, to play to its own progressive gallery.
('Evangelicalism of the Nonconformists' in *Ideas and Beliefs of the Victorians*, p.110)

Was that fine phrase, 'What is morally wrong can never be politically right' the prophetic word, or was it a dangerous catchword which evades the real problem of Christian politics? Long before, Lord Palmerston had said, 'In the long run English politics will follow the conscience of the Dissenters.' He might have added, 'But woe betide them if they try to force the pace.' There is an ominous exultation about the *Methodist Times* for October 1896: 'Sir Charles Dilke defied the Nonconformist conscience and is a political outcast today. Parnell despised the Nonconformist conscience and he destroyed himself and his party. Lord Rosebery ignored the Nonconformist conscience for a racehorse, and the world sees the result.' For the greatest contribution of Nonconformity to English politics was made when it was 'under the Cross' in the seventeenth century and not when, drunk with sight of power, it stooped to employ such boastings as the Gentiles use. (Ibid, pp.111-12)

* * *

All of us live in a world which is being ruthlessly transformed by great tides of history . . . It is part of our trouble that the world of Christian existence has not kept pace. Within the Churches, we move forward, indeed, like the hour-hand of a clock, while outside the world rushes on with the speed of minutes . . .

Our world has had painfully to learn that beliefs can matter catastrophically. If we will not listen to theology, then we shall get ideology, or we shall simply relax on the mental reflexes of some party line. In this age of pre-fabricated thinking there are plenty of Christian groups who will supply our thinking for us at cut prices. There are the 'Fifty shilling mental tailors' who will provide ready-made mental suits of loud and advanced colours, complete with catchwords, jargon, plausible fallacies which will last until the next fashion sets in – the next brand new 'Challenge of . . .' on our discussion programme. Or, if we are more conservative, we can get some second-hand mental clothes and garb our minds with the negative inhibitions, the facile dogmatisms of fading evangelical piety . . .

I believe Wesley's 'Forty-four' are no more out of date than J. S. Bach's equally famous 'Forty-eight', though both need interpreting. Wesley's sermons were no abstract dissertations, but theology as *believed*, theology as *preached*, theology as *sung* . . . Some of them stand sentinel for vital truth, and even where most dated they make excellent astringent medicine for modern Methodists.

('Rethinking Methodism', in *Methodist Recorder*, 28 April 1949)

* * *

21

'Our doctrines' and their technical terms are not isolated units, like the items on a shopping-list. They belong together, like the fieldsmen in a cricket match, where each has his appointed place, and each place its appointed name. That would be a very foolish captain who would dismiss a fieldsman from the field each time a catch was fumbled or a ball dropped. Yet something like this has perhaps been happening with our theology. Some old words, say 'Justification' or 'Total Depravity', have seemed uncouth and we have simply dropped them, with no serious consideration of reliable substitutes, no rearrangement of the field if some such drastic readjustment were necessary.
('The Shape of the Gospel', in *Methodist Recorder*, 26 May, 1949)

* * *

One has the impression that many modern Christians have simply ceased to believe or hope that perfection is the divine goal for them . . . We come so easily to accept the defects of character in fellow-Christians, to suppose that they will never be any different. We become accustomed to the jarring pettinesses which mar our Christian fellowship, we almost expect that five years hence (unless providentially removed elsewhere) the same awkward squad will upset the leaders or the society meeting (Mr Grouser, Mrs 'I-Don't-Want-to-Criticize-But', Mrs Gossip, Mr Righteous Indignation Unconfined, and Mr Speak-the-Truth-without-Love). We have lost the glad assurance that if the Church is a hospital it is a place where, by the Grace of God, cures take place, and where men and women can grow into the mind of Christ towards one another . . .

Those who are always seeking how little they must believe, who reckon each point of doctrine, each precept of discipline, as a fetter and bar upon their minds and hearts, cannot but produce a drab, narrow world of Christian experience, the kind of Christian mediocrity which now prevails, which the outsider rightly finds to be singularly unattractive. To explore one grand truth after another eagerly and expectantly, as part of God's programme for us, as he showers gift upon gift upon us – this is the liberating way which leads us onward where horizon after horizon opens up before us, to that adventure of the saints which is the true catholicity, and will do more than all our discussions and projects towards the mending of the Church and the healing of the world.
('Christian Perfection', in *Methodist Recorder*, 1 December 1949)

1950

The wrath of God as a key to the interpretation of modern history is out of fashion, to be relegated among those categories dismissed by the Master of Trinity as 'pietistic flapdoodle'. The modern historian bids us listen to the story of the past, like a psychiatrist to a patient, resolved above all never to be shocked at what we hear. Yet the Christian must see in the vast upheaval of the sixteenth century an element of judgment.
('Doctrine of Man: the Christian and Secular Eschatology', in *The Expository Times*, Vol. 61, p. 100)

1951

It would be difficult to exaggerate what the Psalter – 'the Bible in miniature' – meant to [Luther]. The Psalms were the first considerable part of the Bible which he got by heart for use in cell and choir. Month by month the Divine offices moved through the Psalter with stately measure, touching the height and depth of every emotion, every mood and almost every human crisis. Now it was the poignant cry of Israel, ravished and discomforted, in exile among her foes; next the exultant joy that God's right arm had swept giant foes into oblivion; the long, backward glances down the corridors of the past, with their reminders against the folly and faithlessness of Israel, of the enduring faithfulness of God. The piteous complaint of the poor man, betrayed, defenceless, while the ungodly struts before him in insolence and pride; the shout of the crowds at some high festival; the impatience of the saints, beset by temptation and anguish; music and dancing, the noisy clamour of the temple courts, the silent eloquence of the little hills, the valleys thick with corn, the great sea, the sun and the stars, the ancient offering of a contrite heart, and through them all the solemn testimony to the transitory glory of this world, against the abiding Word of God.
(*The Progress of Luther to the Diet of Worms*, pp.36-7)

[Luther] could shape a liturgy as well as Thomas Cranmer, though he did not fall into our error of abolishing that variety on which the continuing life of liturgy depends.
(Ibid, p.105)

In the Strand, in London, stands a figure, burly and blunt, reading from a book. It might almost – *mutatis mutandis* – be Luther, but it is Samuel Johnson. The two men had much of their greatness in common,

in their plain common sense, their humour and their melancholy, their delight at shocking their friends, the pathos of their inner struggles, and the loyalty and love they contrived to keep among their friends. Perhaps Luther was less fortunate in the dozen or so inferior Boswells who were permitted to frequent his table and whose garbled and sometimes fuddled remembrances, recorded in the *Table Talk*, are not always faithful and true.[7] But at least we can see Luther and Johnson at home. Nobody ever wore his heart more on his sleeve than Luther, and there for all to see are his fun and tenderness, his deep love of his family and his home, his mighty prayers, and the vulgarity which prevents us thinking of him as some stained-glass figure, or cloying his memory with sickly romanticism. For there are shadows as well as lights.
(Ibid, p.106)

Now, Protestants must be occupied with nothing less than the Reformation of the Reformation itself. The characteristic language, forms, institutions, disciplines, which began four hundred years ago, have come to the end of their journey, as evangelical and pastoral vehicles, however imperishable their value to the trained and instructed within the household of faith. If our gospel is to come home to lost, secular, revolutionary man, the Churches of East and West, Catholic and Protestant, must face the need for creative and drastic change. Within our lifetime new forms of Christian existence may need to arise as different from those of the past as the world of modern Protestantism differs from that of the later Middle Ages . . . Luther bids us look beyond Ecclesiastical Man, even in the guise of prophet and Reformer, to the inspiring prospect of history as the royal progress of the Word of God, going forth conquering and to conquer.
(Ibid, pp.107-8)

* * *

A great community – nation, culture or Church – is a spiritual complexity, the texture of which is as intricate as that of any human body. To examine Methodism within the setting of the Protestant tradition is an operation as delicate as that with which the surgeon's knife must cut between the bone, sinew, nerve and tissue. It is too high for me. I cannot undertake that operation here, though before I have

---

[7]   Cf *The Righteousness of God* (1953), p.6

done many of you may feel I have administered the anaesthetic. All I can do is scrawl a few blackboard comments on the nature of the job, and sketch where, as I think, the incisions should be made.
(*Methodism in Relation to Protestant Tradition*, an address delivered at the Ecumenical Methodist Conference, Oxford 1951, p.9)

When the Reformers attacked Popery, they attacked the intrusion into the holy place of ecclesiastical man, who has bedevilled European history more grievously than political or economic man.
(Ibid, p.12)

That was the age of the pioneers: the sailors, the astronomers, the Reformers. They were followed by the age of the map-makers, who plotted and charted those discoveries, framed them and, giving them a habitation and a name, made it possible for wayfaring men to follow. Such were the Puritans.[8]
(Ibid, p.13)

I have not spoken of the Puritan left. There is something to be said for their version of the four freedoms: freedom from Popery, freedom from bishops, freedom from persecution, and freedom from Presbyterians. For in seventeenth-century England it became clear that the evil of ecclesiastical man was not confined to Popery: that whether bishop or presbyter are the same or different in origin does not matter in the end if they involve an arrogant clericalism which knows no other way with truth than the threefold engine which Christian men bestowed on modern Europe – the closed shop, the Iron Curtain, and the 'party line'. . . Our world, our Christian world, is not yet abreast of Milton's *Areopagitica*: it has not yet learned that neither rack not thumbscrew, branding iron or bullet, cavalry charge or push of pike – nor yet jet fighters and atom bombs – can kill a lie or advance truth one jot or tittle.
(Ibid, p.16)

One of the deadly features of seventeenth-century Protestantism and Catholicism was a one-sided Augustinianism, what M Rondet has called 'a Pessimism of Grace' – the notion that God is only concerned to snatch a tiny handful from the mass of doomed humanity. In contrast was the optimism of Nature of the Rationalist enlightenment. The Arminianism of Wesley had little to do with the academic writings of

---

[8]   In *The Righteousness of God* (1953), p.256 this metaphor is carried a stage further: 'The great pioneers were followed closely by the great map makers, and these in turn gave way to the real epigoni, the map readers.'

Arminius ... It maintained the biblical, Protestant diagnosis of the depth of our human tragedy, which we only realise when we confront the Righteousness of God. But it set 'total grace' over and against 'total sinfulness'; it breathed an optimism of Grace, which changed the whole mood and temper of English Christianity and nerved it for the battle against the giant evils of the coming industrial age.
(Ibid, p.20)

Not only the occasion, but the results of separation [from the Church of England] have to be considered. When we have defended the sincerity of John Wesley and when we have repudiated the discussion in Anglo-Catholic terms, we have still to face the question whether there has not been in consequence a moving away from deep elements in historical Christian continuity, which gave original Methodism a depth and a stability not always evident in later days.
(Ibid, p.23)

In two great centuries, the Elizabethan and the Victorian ages, Protestantism came very close indeed to the conscience of the nation. But it is no accident that 'in all time of our wealth' precedes in the Litany 'in all time of our tribulation'. Here is something which our American friends might care to ponder as we enter the great American century, and where their great Church life flows with the promise of spring – or it might be an Indian summer. We all need to remember Dean Inge's saying that the Church which marries the spirit of the age will be left a widow in the next generation.
(Ibid, p.27)

In these days, when religious publishing houses have made profitable friends with the mammon of unrighteousness, we shall need to support quite firmly our Book Stewards in their fight against the infiltration of unholy custom against the good tradition of our fathers, since the prime object of Methodist publishing is to teach and to evangelize.
(Ibid, p.29)

It is [Protestantism's] strength and weakness that it has always been more apprehensive of new things, closer and more sensitive to the currents of the age and culture through which it moves. That is its strength; but our time affords ugly examples of the weakness whereby a Church succumbs, and becomes adjectival to the spirit of the nation, class, or culture.
(Ibid, p.29)

Let us remember that there has always been much more to the Catholic Church than Popery. And I have sometimes wondered whether the Roman Church is not in these days a praying Church, as large areas of Protestantism have ceased to be! I don't know about a religion fit for scientists, but perhaps a good Protestant religion fit for Hell-deserving sinners, which is all I want to know, might do for scientists, and make them fit for religion, if it were purged of the funk and fudge and fear of truth which again and again has been the poison in our Protestant bloodstream. And we shall need the courage of compassion not to abate one jot or tittle of our social witness. I heard something in America about a 'pink fringe': and it would I think be a mistake to treat Christian left-wing intellectuals as seriously as they take themselves, but do let us remember that the one deadly group in Church history has been the 'yellow fringe' of those who just sit on the fence . . . And when once again we dare to go, not only to those who want us, but to those who want us most, in the dark places of cruelty and the habitations of violence, where we sit in the seat of the scornful and stand in the way of sinners, we shall meet the Lord of the Church already there, standing where He has never ceased to stand in the midst of his broken world bearing its sins, perfectly, sufficiently, and offering the greatest of all his gifts to his chosen people, that they share of the travail of his soul, and may be satisfied.
(Ibid, pp.29-31)

* * *

An 'Ecumenicity' which has no roots in denominational loyalties means in the end a rootless Ecumenical Movement, cut off from the living springs of Christian tradition which are real, existing, worshipping communities of Christian men and women.
('After Oxford? Ecumenical Methodism and the Future' in *London Quarterly & Holborn Review*, July 1951, p.262)

* * *

Not long after the war, I shared a room in Delmenhorst with one of the finest Methodists of our time. He kept by his bedside a small coin. It was a gold dollar, a hundred years old, and it was brought to Germany by the first Methodist to come from American Methodism to Germany. Let that be a parable, reminding us, first, that most of the Methodist work in Europe has originated with our American brethren and is closely linked with their organisation, and second, that, like that tiny gold coin, it has a value and importance out of all proportion to its size. ('Methodist Churches amid Europe's Varied Cultures', in *Methodist Recorder*, 30 August 1951)

1952

There is only one nineteenth-century philosophy of optimism which remains in the field as an active, operative idealism, and that is the Marxist interpretation of history. It is a philosophy which has room for tragedy and conflict and which does more justice to the tragic dynamism of history than the more superficial Christian interpretations of the last hundred years. It is part of our trouble that Western civilization has lost faith in progress, lost faith in the momentum of the good just at the very time when it cannot, if it would, escape the consequences of the dynamic of evil. We are paying the price of wishful and superficial thinking.
(*Principalities and Powers*, p.20)

A great deal of what counts for prophetic speaking, even in the ecumenical movement, is set in the minor key and lacks anything of the resilient courage which nerved the great Christians of the nineteenth century to their victorious assaults upon evil.
(Ibid, p.21)

We can make sense of that part of our history of which we are victims only if we recognize that other part of which we are villains. And perhaps only those who see over and against the world one like unto the Son of Man, their Conqueror and their King, can face all the facts about man and the world.
(Ibid, p. 22)

Then there is the all-important distinction between history as it took place, once for all, in the past, and history as it has been written down, recorded, and remembered. History as it really happened is man minding his own business; history as recorded and remembered is glorified eavesdropping and it is after all a very chancy affair. We have rescued only a tiny fragment of the past, and we cannot guarantee that the really significant facts have not been lost. It is as though we tried to reconstruct the life, character and habits of the five thousand by examining the contents of the twelve baskets of fragments which remained. When primitive men ages ago burned and destroyed some

lakeside settlement they did what they did for their own rough purposes, but we may be sure that they had no idea that they were destroying valuable historical evidence, and they were not halted in their cruel operation by the reflection that they were making things much harder for the editors of the *Cambridge Ancient History*!
(Ibid, p.26)

Consider the very proportions of the Gospel narratives. Within this single life they slip rapidly over thirty years. They fasten on rather less than three years, and within this period on a few months, and within this one week, and then finally on events in two days which are evidently conceived to be of such importance that they are described to us, hour by hour. We get the kind of sensation we know when we have been riding through the countryside in an express train and when the brakes have been applied, and we have slowed down, slower, slower still, until at last with a screech of brakes the train has jerked to a halt and to silence. So history slows down in the Gospels until at last all history moves from action to passion and jerks to a halt before the three hours silence of Jesus on His Cross.
(Ibid, p.32)

The plan of salvation is less like a thin red line running through the centuries than a stone flung into a pond, from which the ripples extend in all directions.
(Ibid, p.33)

The word *homoousios* in the Nicene Creed has tested thought many times through many centuries. Its background is complex, but compared with it the great New Testament *dikaiosune*, righteousness, looks down like a giant redwood upon some upstart sapling planted in its shade.
(Ibid, p.37)

History is a hostess who takes in some very strange lodgers, and who often shocks our moral sense by not asking too many questions about the character of those she entertains. The power of ideas in human history does not seem to depend on their truth or falsity . . . Ideas which suddenly find terrifying lodgement in a historical situation do not need to be true or new or good.
The ideologies of modern revolutionary man provide the most startling illustration of this. The half-baked theories of Houston Stewart Chamberlain, of Rosenberg's *Twentieth Century Myth*, of Adolf Hitler's *Mein Kampf,* were so childish, so fatally easy to refute at the academic

level, that we entirely misunderstood their danger. For these ideas took root like evil seed in a good soil. They battened on the idealism of youth, the surging energies of a great nation. Nobody who lived in Germany in 1936 could doubt that the Nazi creed was something hailed with enthusiasm and joy by millions of young people who were prepared to make all manner of costly and adventurous sacrifices on its behalf. We should be very foolish indeed if we ignored that fact that the same enthusiasm, the same sense of having found a purposeful, liberating, and joyous religion, is shared by millions of young men and women behind the Iron Curtain in lands we too easily misconceive as groaning with discontents and only longing for liberation without . . . We go very far astray if we think we have met the problem of Marxist communism when we have met its arguments at the academic level, and we shall go very much further astray if we imagine that its influence on our world will bear any necessary relation to the truth or falsity of its ideas. The stuff of history supports the evil and the good, and is far closer to the realism of Machiavelli than the simple moralism of John Wesley.
(Ibid, pp.43-5)

It is part of this Christian hope of ours to know that the lies and hatred and lust and fears are the weak things, that the stars in their courses are on the side of mercy and of truth.
(Ibid, p.58)

It is a valid criticism of every secular Utopianism that the goal becomes emptied of meaning as we approach it. To get to it the rest of history becomes a means to an end; the ages are turned into a vast escalator where it is only the final step which counts, and all the other steps are deprived of meaning. And the rest of mankind have no guarantee that all their sweat and blood and tears will not have been in vain, since they have no guarantee that the last generation will not decide to switch ideals and go in for something else, or to fling shamelessly away the travail of the ages.
(Ibid, pp.71-2)

A few years ago a shop stood in the Strand in London close by Charing Cross Railway Station. It sold the kind of cheap presents, souvenirs of London, which trippers and visitors might be expected to buy. When I first saw it, its windows were splashed with red banner advertisements, 'Positively the Last Few Days, Closing Sale!' I was amazed when I went by there a few months later to find it still open, but with a clean new set of posters equally startling and impressive, proclaiming, 'Positively the Last Few Days, Closing Sale!' And six months later it was still apparently in the act of closing. And then I understood and in my heart commended this unjust steward. He knew what effect these posters would have on visitors from the country . . . Then came the London Blitz, and one morning I found that shop a mass of debris. Well, I thought, you asked for that. You've had it. But no! A week later I went by, and over the ruins there were new posters, 'Positively the Last Few Days, Great Salvage Sale!'

Isn't that a parable of the Early Church in the world and of what eschatology means? Did not the Church say to that age, 'Now make up your mind. Tomorrow may be too late. Positively the last few days.' And so each moment became of infinite consequence for Christian decision . . . For each of us, this very moment, this now is the edge of history. God's plan of salvation in history is today, if you will hear His voice.
(Ibid, pp.74-5)

It is possible for people to go on for quite a time doing the right things for the wrong reasons. This is the genius of the Anglo-Saxons. We have a gift for it. It is perhaps preferable to the German faculty for seeking the most profound reasons at an immense depth of truth and postponing all action until it has been related to the *Weltanschauung*. It is not irrelevant to notice that the German Protestant Churches from 1848 onward produced a coherent and integrated theology of social action in the writings of Eichern, Lohmann, and Naumann, and one that compares more than favourably with that of the Christian Socialists and the Nonconformist Liberals of Victorian England. But the results were vastly different. The British acted and thought out as they went along, and the results have been written in history. The German thinkers allowed their brave ideals to become stifled, and the results have been written in history of a sadly different kind. Nevertheless, it would be disastrous for Christians to enter the coming age with bewildered minds, and to carry forward programmes for society based upon a discredited and one-sided theology.
(Ibid, pp.95-6)

Modern man turns to the Church for some courageous word in the light of great economic and sociological pressures, but there can be no word from the Church or to the Christian world if we refuse to heed the word which stands over us already: 'Take heed, and beware of covetousness: for a man's life consisteth not in the abundance of things which he possesseth.' Modern man is afraid, for he knows that men have it in their power to make an end of all earthly human existence.

And he looks to the Church for a prophetic word, but there will be no prophetic word given to our churches or to our Christian world until we have learned the word which stands over us already: 'Fear not them which can kill the body, but are not able to kill the soul: but rather fear him which is able to destroy both soul and body in hell.' Western civilization would much rather come to terms with the Church than with Jesus. But he will not be brushed aside. 'He stands upon his cue, and his voice is imperial.' . . . History is a warning of the ruthless judgments of history upon Christian complacency.
(Ibid, p.99)

1953

We must never forget that until the 1830s the Church of England was far nearer to the Middle Ages than to our modern world, and that in her structure the old frustrating abuses lingered which, on the Continent, had been swept away by the Counter Reformation.
('Some Reflections on the Origin and Development of the English Methodist Tradition, 1738-1898', in *London Quarterly and Holborn Review*, 1953, p.167)

One listens to the Ecumenical conversation with sureness that the Methodist contribution must not go by default as, by and large, it seemed to do at Amsterdam. We heard there, on the one side, the old optimism of nature, the humanist evaluation of man, nature and history tricked out under a Christian veneer worn desperately thin. We heard on the other side the pessimism of Grace, the stern call to the remnant to be faithful in the Church 'under the Cross'. Only the Jesuits who were not there, and the Methodists might have spoken of that optimism of Grace, of hope for the whole of mankind, of the power of faith to the casting-down of strongholds, of the salvation of myriads, of the mending of the Churches, and the healing of the nations by the Catholic spirit, the royal way of love.
(Ibid, pp.174-5)

1954

[Thomas Jackson] was perhaps, though certainly not the last, newly appointed Tutor to dread most of all the questions which would be fired at him, well-aimed shafts, as he anticipated, piercing the very joints of

32

his harness, and to forestall in imagination the awful moment when his blushful, stammering ignorance would be publicly displayed. He was also not the last to discover that this particular nightmare, so common as almost to qualify as an industrial disease, was singularly removed from reality.
(*Thomas Jackson, Methodist Patriarch*, p.28)

. . . the great questions which have busied the minds of those Christian thinkers who have made Christian theology to date the most sustained piece of high-level corporate thinking in the history of mankind.
(Ibid, p.31)

Great are the temptations which come when Satan appears as an angel of light; but the most sinister of all temptations to the Church is that which comes, as it came to the Wesleyans and Roman Catholics in the nineteenth century, when the angel of light is disguised as Satan, and when the call of divine truth, divine compassion and divine justice is unheard and unheeded, because it is imbedded in an ideology atheistic, unChristian, anti-clerical, and profane.
(Ibid, p.39)

Our present zeal to compass sea and land to achieve one Ph.D. is of doubtful value to the cause of lasting scholarship; I suspect the reason for the mediocrity of so many historical and theological theses is that they are coveted, not as the beginning, but as the end of study.
(Ibid, p.50)

I know the perils of antiquarianism. But I have seen enough trivial libraries of men who have never kept up reading, and whose middle ministry has ended in shallows and in miseries, and I have heard enough sermons from them, to know that there are worse perils than too much reading; and in any case I should be more wary of those who walk noisily abroad among us in the mental clothes of the Edwardians (1907 or 1937) than of those who have learned to understand the thought world of King James or of the first Queen Elizabeth.
(Ibid, p.51)

* * *

The doctrine of the Word, in the first age of the Reformation, was a rich and many-sided concept, more like a chord of music than a single note. In Luther the doctrine is closely knit with a rich doctrine of the Holy Spirit. But one of the results of the strains and stresses set up within the Reformation from 1522 onwards is the gradual splitting apart of the twin concepts of the Word and Spirit, until on the one hand an over-emphasis on the Outward Word led to a narrowing Biblicism or an equation of the Word with 'pure doctrine', while on the other, a conception of the Inner Word, and of the operation of the Spirit, led to subjectivism and fanaticism. It was not least among the theological achievements of John Calvin that he re-united these great concepts in a doctrine of the Word which gave due room for the operation and the testimony of the Holy Spirit.
(*Prophetic Preaching*, pp.7-8)

I do not suppose Amos would have done very well in the B.D. examination. I remember with reverence how simple was the furnishing of the mind of Jesus. Sometimes theological teachers seem concerned to construct elaborate electronic machines when the need is really for skylarks. But a Methodist preacher cannot get John Wesley out of his system and he will hardly believe that there can be a sustained ministry of preaching, which deepens with the ripening years, without much hard work, without a mental discipline and continuous study which requires all the grace and all the wits we have.
(Ibid, p.13)

Even in the Old Testament there is a connection between the Prophet and the whole People of God. The prophetic burdens of Amos, Isaiah, Jeremiah, Ezekiel may have been handed down by faithful bands of prophetic disciples, but they themselves survived within the whole community of Israel. Naturally the sharpness of the prophetic teaching is blurred within the greater whole. Most of us at Church bazaars have plunged our hand into a bucket of water, to pick up a sixpence from the bottom. It was not only the electric current which was the difficulty, but that we forgot to allow for the refracting and distorting medium of the water, and so we misjudged depth and direction. It is so with the voice of the official Church. Great communities of millions of men and women move and think slowly, they acquire a great moral inertia, find it always easier to relax in terms of some earlier ethical pattern. And besides this, there is the greatest of all non-theological factors, Original Sin. And so we chafe at some document ('Just one clitch after another,'

as the lady said) which emerges from this or that commission, and we groan when what began with a triumphant 'We have the mind of Christ' emerges from the process known as corporate thinking as a doleful 'Who has believed our Report?' and our consolation is that in a few months it will all be safely buried in the Minutes of the Methodist Conference or in some similar decorous graveyard. Not that we should despise these things, for in the end men get more food from our platitudes than from our paradoxes, only they are not prophetic speaking.
(Ibid, p.14)

The prophet is distinguished from the false prophet (and how much of the Old Testament illuminates the point) in that he does not simply echo the spirit of the age, does not simply tell men what they want to hear (what often they already know). But he must beware lest he fall into the opposite error, of supposing that some rebel pattern, which cuts across majority opinion, is not also prefabricated and culturally conditioned, [but] is a word of the Lord to be accepted without criticism, and without submission to the Inquisition of the Biblical dimension . . . The false prophet is no less false if he exchanges playing to the gallery for playing to the dress circle, by playing court chaplain to King Demos. Prefabricated thinking, even at an advanced level, cannot lead to prophetic preaching, but only to sectarian agitation, bitterness and fanaticism . . . I should not care to define a fanatic unless it be one who preaches the sour milk of the Gospel.
(Ibid, pp.15-16)

Compassion makes the prophetic preacher give the devil his due, and seek the facts of the causes he defends and the opponents he combats. The most futile of all the current substitutes for prophetic preaching is the type of sermon on 'Christianity and . . .' which consists of a series of ventriloquial conversations (in the pulpit) with hastily constructed dummies labelled Communism, Atheism, Existentialism, Logical Positivism and the like.
(Ibid, p.16)

But now, when so many millions are estranged from organised religion, we must remember that the prophetic vocation of the Church is bound up with its priestly office. Nagging at the Nation, recalling it to moral principles, with solemn warnings of judgment to come, or already made manifest, may result in the still greater isolation of the Churches themselves, walled off behind their decent proprieties. The Church has only a right to speak over and against the nation, if it is there already: if

it exists there, which is far better, in the multitudes of its own members and in a ministry which shares the joys and sorrows, hopes and fears of the men and women around it; if it establishes Christian listening posts at every place of deep human need and social pressure; or if it goes there in intervention, compassionate, costly, personal, by which Christian men prove the things they say by the patent service of their lives in sustained drudgery and patient sacrifice.
(Ibid, p.17)

Nuremberg in 1947 was not a nice place. The hotels were full of the hangers-on of the terrible War Crimes Trial then going on. One afternoon I climbed over the rubble of medieval Nuremberg, and the massed graves from which men and women had never been dug after the gigantic air raids, and as we passed the lovely Sebaldus Kirche, my driver drew my attention to the figure of Christ carved upon the wall. It was Christ the King, crowned upon his Cross. But the crown of thorns was almost grotesque, double the thickness of any crown of thorns I had ever seen: and the nails in His hands and feet were great shafts of metal. It seemed to me on reflection a prophetic symbol. There it had stood, this carving, for long centuries until the air raids, until those nights of unimaginable horror and pain – double pain: there it had waited until a few hundred yards away there was broadcast from the courthouse the vile story of human inhumanity, cruelty and guilt, double guilt: and in the place of double pain and double guilt there stood in the midst of lost humanity its Prophet, Priest and King, comforting His people as only He can comfort, He who is the true Israel and who has received double for all her sins. Prophetic preaching is preaching according to this measure: according to the measure of the stature of the fulness of Christ.
(Ibid, p.18)

* * *

We think of the past as stretching behind us, much as the wake of an ocean liner fades into the distance, but it has been suggested that perhaps we should think of other centuries as swinging on their orbits like so many planets, and that every now and again one particular century appears in close conjunction with the present. So it is with the sixteenth century and our own age.
(*Manchester Guardian*, 20 September 1954)

John Buchan's 'Mr Standfast' . . . fulfilled the office of middleman for me, to initiate me into Bunyan's writings as a never-failing spring of profit, wonder and joy.

Of course, the *Progress* does not take to summarising. Analyse the story as the allegory of the soul and it becomes dull, banal, a trip to Italy as if described in Bradshaw. For Bunyan's greatness was that of Dante, the eyes that saw everything and the humour which delighted to watch our common life, the same insight and the same humour, we may reverently believe, which gave us the Parables of the Gospels.

Mr Sharrock[9] gives the second part of the *Progress* its due: he does not repeat the stupid fallacy that sequels are always a failure (any theologian will tell you that all the best quotations in *Alice* come from *Through the Looking Glass*). There is nothing in the first part which for gentle humour matches Christiana giving medicine to her naughty boys (unless it be the very subtle mastery with which Giant Despair is portrayed as a hen-pecked husband) or with the reverberating beauties, nay, the majesty of the closing passages of the work.

(Ibid, 18 October 1954)

1955

In a way, it was easier for Norwegian, French or Dutch Christians to resist the Nazis, for they could do so as good patriots. It was harder for the Germans, and I remember being told in 1937 in Germany that men like Niemoller were simply 'bad Germans'. There is no point in ignoring a widespread Christian failure at this point. Luther's subtle and profound teaching about the State had been over-simplified and misunderstood in later generations, and the course of German history itself – which I regard as the real villain of the piece – ended in a situation where too many Christians were only too ready to leave the State to its own devices, and tamely to insist only on the duty of obedience . . .

So often, when people ask, 'Why doesn't the Church give a lead?', they think in terms of official pronouncements by official bodies. I have always thought it rather simple to expect heroic or prophetic initiative from such quarters. Great institutions, composed of many millions of men and women, think slowly, acquire a certain moral inertia, find it always easier to relax on some older moralistic pattern

9   Roger Sharrock, author of *John Bunyan* (1954).

than to apprehend a new situation, and the prophetic quality may easily be lost in the machinery of the modern ecclesiastical bureaucracy, and the pulling and tearing machine of ecclesiastical party politics. Ecclesiastical pronouncements almost always say too much, do too little, and come too late: though every now and then, when an ecclesiastical dignitary ventures to shake loose a gaiter in a moment of calculated indiscretion, we have every reason to be grateful for it . . . [But] we shall be wise to take these things for what they are, and not simply to criticise them as though this were the voice of the 'Church', as though this absolved the rest of us, lay folk as well as parsons, and – dare one say it? – university dons, from the tiresome, mucky discipline of thinking in and with and through the Church as humble and yet responsible members.

One may wonder whether it is the duty of the Church always to go against the stream, whether a kind of 'see what Johnny is doing and tell him not to' attitude is not just as un-Christian as to be a perpetual 'yes-man', and whether in fact the perpetual 'no-man' is really not a prophet, but a fanatic, that well-known but rather unattractive figure, the professional ecclesiastical rebel? . . .

I have not tried to minimise or explain away Christian failure. But I believe that, beyond this, there has been a Christian achievement. In the history of 2,000 years Christian innocence has shown a stubborn core. The Babes in the Wood turn out to be rather tough babies, almost as tough as the infants in the cartoons of Giles or Ronald Searle. And we might remember that, in the story, the wood came to belong to the Babes in the end, and that the Wicked Uncles of history have been, in the exact and biblical sense of the word, the political fools.
('The Two Kingdoms', in *The Listener*, 3 March 1955)

*   *   *

Like Puritanism [Victorian Nonconformity] has often been caricatured, and, like all caricatures, there is a great truth in the exaggeration. But, like Puritanism, it had a massive strength. It shared with Puritanism a civilising framework, the religion of the home, of Sunday, of the Bible, and a moralism centred on religious fervour . . . I need not stress how it could go wrong: the casualties of Victorian religion are still with us, in the estrangement of millions from organised religion of any kind. A 'Big Brother is watching you' kind of God: the preoccupation with death and the possibility of hell, a narrowed and departmentalised Biblical horizon classically portrayed in Gosse's *Father and Son* . . .

That startling Christian radicalism, which is for ever turning the world upside down by putting little people in mind of ineffable and eternal dignities, was at work with long-term results written large in the history of the trade union and socialist movements, even though Methodism failed to become, in fact, the Established Church of Disraeli's 'other nation'.

[The 'Nonconformist conscience'] If the eclipse of political Puritanism in the seventeenth century and of Victorian Nonconformity in the nineteenth are reminders of the inevitable reaction against the attempt of moralists to force the pace and carry through a programme by a moral force which rides over an unconvinced and unconverted majority, there is another side. There was the valiant stand for public and private integrity, for principle as against expediency. Above all, there was the concern for the whole of life.
('The Influence of Victorian Nonconformity', in *The Listener*, 17 March 1955)

* * *

The Puritan knew that the good fight of faith is lonely and vehement, that the front line of the whole Christian warfare runs through the conscience of the individual, that here all is at stake. But beginning there he adventured into a pattern of social ethics, expressed in a notable literature of devotion and of casuistry . . . If history has not done justice to the Puritans, it may be that they did not do justice to themselves, and that they overlaid with narrow pieties and fustian integuments a great weight of solid integrity and heroic Christian virtue . . .

In the end, ignorance is no excuse, for Christian charity involves a compassionate inquisitiveness. 'I like to ask questions and to see things for myself,' explained the Bishop of Chichester in Berlin in 1945 to his somewhat breathless conductors, as he bustled them from one foetid refugee shelter, one spot of devastated, desolate agony, to another . . .

Without charity, all our deeds and all our speeches are worth nothing, but given this divine sustaining energy, immense creative and renewing forces are available to the Christian Community which in the past have moved history, and will move it ever and again. Our paganized generation may have forgotten most Christian truths, but it has remembered sufficient to judge our words by our deeds, and to measure them both by the example of Him who bestrides history as Prophet, Priest, and King. It will not go unheedful of the Church which

takes upon itself the form of a servant, and is ready, if need be, to lay down its life for the sheep.
('The Christian Community: creating public conscience', a Cambridge University sermon; *London Quarterly & Holborn Review*, July 1955, pp.223-6)

* * *

There are fashions in theology as in clothes, and the latest contrivances of our theological Schiaparellis, Diors and Hartnells become the rage among the students, and more than they will often admit, the preachers and the teachers. Now and again some word like 'Basingstoke' in *Ruddigore* teems with hidden meaning for the initiated, but becomes a snare indeed for bewildered and puzzled congregations at the mercy of the woolly-minded theological student or preacher obeying the unwritten rubric, 'When in doubt say "Eschatology" or "Demythologising" or "Biblical Theology".'
(*Manchester Guardian*, 2 May 1955)

[*After a visit by Billy Graham to Cambridge*] Mr Graham has shown an open-mindedness, a sincere tolerance, an appreciation of the many-sidedness of truth, a genuine catholicity bursting its limitations which has not been the hallmark of Cambridge evangelical student bodies in recent years, and the visit will have been well worth while if it converts the temper of the sponsoring body, and if henceforth it is not so much 'loudly' as 'sweetly' sing C.I.C.C.U. ... As one whose gratitude to Mr Graham can best be expressed by sharpening one's intellectual armament still more against a narrow and intolerant pietism, banefully resurgent in our universities, and as one who covets for his university an evangelism frank and sincere and cogent, but at an altogether different level of intellectual awareness and understanding from the estranged mind of our time, I should judge that, in default of a William Temple, Mr Billy Graham has done us very well.
(Ibid, 14 November 1955)

1956

The qualities of character which go to make a Christian man go also to make a proper historian. There is a discipline of spirit in all the intellectual pursuits, but in that of the student and teacher of history there is the most demanding of all – the blending of love for truth with the insights of charity. The study of history will not give a man

qualities of character which he does not already possess, or cannot win from the battle of faith in daily life; but it will give him timely lessons, and will continually call old worlds into being to redress the balance of the new.
(The Christian Use of History', in *An Approach to Christian Education*, p.97)

* * *

We need not romanticize the mantle of Elijah. It was no doubt a plain, homespun, utility affair. In an age which rated cleanliness far, far below godliness, it must have had much in common with that old, verminous sheepskin which was the famous legacy to St Athanasius of great Antony of Egypt. But it, too, was an emblem of a partnership between generations. Today a man may stare through a glass darkly, in the museum of San Marco in Florence, at the mantle of that medieval prophet, Jerome Savonarola; yet it is remote, cut off, a museum piece from which all virtue has long ago departed. But, in the moment of parting between this great master and this great disciple, the mantle of Elijah was a portent, a sign and a wonder . . .

Dr Wilbert Howard told me once how when he was a boy he went visiting with his father in a new circuit, and they stopped to talk with an old local preacher. He never forgot how the old cobbler suddenly produced from under his bench a Greek New Testament and a Hebrew Bible, and how he watched the two men read together. Ah, but then the Superintendent of that circuit had been the great Dr Etheridge, who had held a class which met a six o'clock in the morning so that the lay preachers might possess the grand tools of the sacred languages. And then Dr Etheridge had been the disciple as well as the biographer of Adam Clarke, that splendid, lovable genius, master of eighteen languages, who travelled with his Hebrew, Greek, and Latin Bibles in a case slung round his neck. And Adam Clarke it was who kneeled down in a vestry in Bristol while his great hero, John Wesley, commissioned him to preach our doctrines. That is the [prophetic] succession I have in mind. And, if we take into account this living memory of great teachers, how it lights up the appeal to tradition in the second century – St Irenaeus bursting out when he mentions Polycarp: 'We too saw him in our youth, for he lived a long time, having always taught the things he had learned from the Apostles'; or Papias taking note of what his contemporaries had learned from the very Apostles; and behind these, the greater voices of St John, St Peter, and St Paul (for we may indeed believe that behind the Pauline Corpus there were men whose faces glowed when they spoke of Paul, as I have seen men whose faces lit up

41

when they spoke of Ryder Smith and Alec Findlay and Dr Lofthouse, to come no nearer home) . . .

We must, of course, take the theology of a past age with discrimination as well as with imagination. This autumn season reminds us of the dead weight of leaves which every year must die, after their little day, and of the fact that even of the seeds which fall to the ground, very few will have survival value. But the seeds are there. This is specially true of the vast literature of seventeenth-century Puritanism, that ferment of thought which produced 22,000 pamphlets between 1640 and 1660 and innumerable tomes of moral and spiritual theology. There are dead leaves enough there. Oh (to Americanize) what a Fall was there, my countrymen! Wild horses would not make me read the daunting volumes of Charnock on the 'Divine Attributes'. If in our day some new John Wesley should fall in love with some new Sophy Hopkey, I cannot imagine his saying, as did our father: 'Let's find a quiet spot – and read the works of Dr John Owen.' And yet, the rediscovery of Puritanism, led by the American historians, has important things to say to us about the meaning of a Christian Church or a Christian society, and about a genuinely Protestant moral theology and devotional literature . . .

It would be unfair, and at least an exaggeration, but I have sometimes thought that a new Max Beerbohm might draw a cartoon of this mid-twentieth century scene by showing excited theologians dancing round broken vessels in a dark cave beside the Dead Sea, while the scientists try to explode the universe in another part of the desert! (From a sermon on 2 Kings 2:11, preached at Handsworth Theological College; in *London Quarterly & Holborn Review*, April 1956, pp.134-8)

* * *

I write this for the select band of Philistines who are wont to write in the margins of their books. Give us a new book, a pencil and a fire and we are well set to feel the glow of elevated thoughts, which, with incredible compression, we distill into an exclamation or a question mark, and now and then a pithy comment, nasty, brutish, short or adulatory as may be. Ours is an honorary pedigree going back to the first printed books, to the ruderies of the young Luther in his copy of Gabriel Biel and the inspired doodlings of Holbein in his copy of *The Praise of Folly*. Addicts will know our special temptations. One book is after all much like another and the problem is bound to arise sooner or later of other people's books. S. T. Coleridge, who was wont to embellish not only volumes belonging to his friends, but those

belonging to circulating libraries, reminds us that in the matter of book behaviour it is sadly but strangely true that the godly and upright are wont to display what Kierkegaard called a 'teleological suspension of ethics' in a moral area not yet investigated by the Nonconformist conscience.
(*Manchester Guardian*, 6 February 1956)

Let those of us who think of plugging into the living Catholic tradition of the ancient churches remember about episcopacy as much else, that the light switch is more important than the power switch, and that authority and dominion and administration are irrelevant beside the guardianship of truth, the wholeness of the Gospel, and the will of God that his Church should show forth to men and women the Form of a Servant.
(Ibid, 30 April 1956)

* * *

I suppose in the next years the Methodist Conference will be invited to pass thousands of resolutions upon every subject in heaven and on earth, and the result of this incessant battering of epigrams into platitudes will by the end of the decade be peacefully entombed in the volumes of the *Minutes of Conference* without the world being any the wiser, or the worse.
(Address delivered at the World Methodist Conference at Lake Junaluska)

We shall so strengthen our links with World Methodism that we shall achieve that catholicity which alone can safeguard separate churches from becoming submerged by culture, class or nation – though I hope we shall remember that a World Sect, a Methodist International dominated by English and American bureaucrats, exempt from disciplinary safeguards, might be a very horrid thing, more detestable, it may be, than that other World Sect of the Bishop of Rome and all his enormities.
(Ibid)

* * *

It is important for the historian that he should exercise a salutary scepticism towards his materials and his sources, but even more important that he should adopt this detachment towards himself, and when confronted by apparent confusion and contradiction in some great

figure of the past, to ask whether perhaps he himself as historian may be asking the wrong questions, and evaluating another century in the themes and categories of a later age.
('Luther and the Doctrine of the Church', in *Scottish Journal of Theology*, 1956, p.384)

The modern professional historian is singularly unhandy with theology, and especially Protestant theology, and only too eager to plunge into the foggy categories of psychology or religious experience. (Ibid, pp.384-5)

* * *

In the National Gallery there is a famous painting of the 'Adoration of the Kings'. It was painted by Peter Breughel, who lived in the middle of the sixteenth century, at a time when his native Low Countries were overrun by the cruel soldiery of Imperial Spain. Mary and her baby, Joseph and the shepherds are drawn with peasant realism; but the background is thronged with soldiers, pressing close to the Holy Family. As Mary stretches out her hand towards the royal gifts of the Three Kings she almost touches a crossbow, while a tall pike, held in mailed fist, rises above her head.

'He breaketh the bow: he cutteth the spear in sunder.' Does he? the picture seems to ask. Sixteen centuries have passed and the men of violence possess the earth, and still the poor and innocent are oppressed. In the foreground kneel two of the Kings, and it is they who have won for this picture the name of the 'most cynical painting in the world'. For though they have come to Bethlehem, it is plain that self-interest has brought them together, and they glance uneasily at one another. At the side of the picture (a modern enough touch, this!) the African waits patiently to bring his gift when the white men have done.

This Christmas I feel grateful to Peter Breughel for the realism of this picture. It matches our time, for the new Cambridge Modern History entitles the story of our lifetime, 'The Era of Violence', and in the last days we have heard again the noise of armour, the armed man in tumult, and the garments rolled in blood. We need not only the realism of Bethlehem itself, the historicity of the fact of Jesus of Nazareth, but the remembrance that he entered all the context of our human existence, all those pressures of history and environment, all the tangle of human sin, was born 'under the Law', and amid it all, free and innocent. And the question put by Breughel is expressed in the words which Dorothy Sayers puts into the mouth of Melchior – 'Love and power are always at war together. And the riddle that torments the world is this: Shall

Power and Love dwell together at last, when the promised Kingdom comes?' . . .

I remember a summer day outside Durban in South Africa, at the opening of a clinic for Africans which had been built in the midst of one of those festering shanty towns, a generous gift from the white Christians, the money raised by a Methodist Men's Fellowship, and the services of a lady doctor generously given. Unexpectedly, the meaning of that day was summed up when a choir of Africans stood and sang from the Psalms, 'Blessed is he that considers the poor and needy: the Lord shall consider him in time of trouble.' And I have wondered often since whether this blessing of white brethren by the Poor of Africa for the sake of Livingstone, Schweitzer and many other good Christian people, may not be a mighty if imponderable thing, something which challenges the rest of us with the thought that, despite our fine missionary record, we have cared too little and too late.

Let us not sentimentalize about the Christmas story this year. But let us see it in its grim and painful realism, as it matches our world, and as it speaks across our tidy, ordered, civilized life to the dark places where the refugees still tread the weary road and halt to hear the soldiery of Herod.

(Christmas sermon, in *Methodist Recorder*, 6 December 1956)

1957

We need not apologise for what we now politely call 'non-theological factors' but which might more bluntly be called 'original sin' and not at all original cussedness . . .

. . . factors which might be defined as environment worked over by original sin.

(*Luther Today*, pp.108, 148)

We must not think of the Reformation as though Martin Luther were the norm, and all else deviation from the Lutheran party line. For it is really Luther who is the great surprise . . . Luther is disconcerting, with his heights and depths of exploration of the Biblical world, his poised and balanced Middle Way between Popery and Puritanism, a more genuine 'Via Media' than the Anglican muddle of principle and expediency . . . But for him, Puritanism would have swallowed up Protestantism, and the whole matter of the Reformation might have been dissolved in a new legalism in religion, and in sectarian strife.

(Ibid, p.109)

[Carlstadt] was that not unknown phenomenon, the 'coming man' who somehow fails to emerge, the *enfant terrible* who refuses to grow up and in whom originality sours into eccentricity. Most theological faculties have at some time or other to contend with these academic Peter Pans.
(Ibid, p.111)

[Carlstadt] startled his students one morning by addressing them as 'My dear colleagues'. They had heard of the Priesthood of All Believers, but had not heard until now of what might be called the 'Vice Chancellorship of All Undergraduates'.
(Ibid, p.120)

Andrew Carlstadt and Thomas Muntzer really were 'wild men'. They were genuine archetypes of what Luther called *Schwarmerei* (which might be defined as 'too many bees chasing too few bonnets').
(Ibid, p.147)

A few months ago in a broadcast to the Russian Zone of Germany, which was later broadcast to Moscow on the BBC, I suggested that it was not Luther who in 1525 'let the peasants down', but Thomas Muntzer with his utopian pipe dreams and his dialectical thinking which led only to terrible disillusionment and disaster. But may I close with what I also said then? 'Strange, unhappy, perverted, fanatical, Muntzer was all these things, and it is easy enough to demonstrate them. And yet in him, as in almost no other figure, we come near to that smothered medieval undercurrent of injustice, resentment and pain, now defeated once more, now driven dangerously underground – a tradition lost to the Church but one day to return to the gates of Christendom – aggressive, heretical, anticlerical, yet a witness somewhere to a Christian failure of practical compassion. Thomas Muntzer, like the Iron Curtain, should give us an uneasy conscience.'
(Ibid, p.145-6)

A century and a half of religious warfare was to count more than all the sins of the medieval church towards the estrangement of modern man from organized religion.
(Ibid, p.163)

[*Muntzer at Allstedt, 'a small community of a few hundred near the mining areas of Mansfeld'*] These little communities offered plenty of scope for lawless spirits. If we want a modern parallel to Muntzer and his friends, we had better not think of Marx and Engels working quietly among the manuscripts of the British Museum, but rather of the Wild West some generations ago, of Jesse James and the 'Daltons ride again'. (Ibid, p. 132-3)

* * *

Protestantism was born with the doctrine of the Priesthood of all Believers; it may die unless it discovers the Priesthood of Unbelievers, its solidarity with all men everywhere, and with the great High Priest who died with undistinguishing regard for all mankind and who ever liveth to make intercession for them.
('Methodism in relation to the Protestant World' in *London Quarterly & Holborn Review*, January 1957, p.11)

* * *

God sometimes honours his servants by accepting the price of their renunciations. When, along the winding road from Quy to Cambridge, under a stormy sky, the young Methodist divine renounced his 'philosophical and theological ambitions', that he might live among the London poor and demonstrate the practical power of Christian compassion in the darkest city of Victorian England, he counted a cost which, in fact, he paid. Henceforth the main energies of his virile frame and powerful intellect were diverted into other channels. Because he did in fact achieve intellectual eminence and renown, because no less than four great Universities honoured him with a doctor's degree in theology, we must not forget the price of his supreme vocation of public service. Because of it, the name of Scott Lidgett occupies less room in histories of Christian thought in the nineteenth century, though the more brightly written in heaven.
('The Biblical Theologian', in *John Scott Lidgett: A Symposium*, 1957, p.81)

[In the later nineteenth century] converging streams of new knowledge burst upon an unprepared orthodoxy, whose first reaction, naturally enough, was to go on the defensive, but whose fatal betrayal was to stay there. What had previously been virile, liberating impulses and intuitions, propounded by great minds and spiritual giants, had become cramped, rigid patterns of moralistic pietism. The new learning, in the nineteenth as in the sixteenth century, was not simply new information, but new methodologies, new ways of looking at the world as it is, and the past as it may have been, involving flexible

adjustments of mind and spirit, not only towards the world of nature and history, but to the great imponderables of the invisible world.
(Ibid, p.82)

The Victorian age of giants produced also giant Christians. Men might attack Christian doctrines and exclaim at apparent crudities in ancient orthodoxies, but they could not sneer at the mental and spiritual bankruptcy of Churches which produced a Newman, a Maurice, and a Dale. They might bring the partly justified charge of an other-worldly pietism against the Churches, but they could not press it right home to a generation which remembered Wilberforce, honoured Lord Shaftesbury, and heeded the passionate preaching of Charles Kingsley. Amid the hubbub about the Bible, there rose the mighty Cambridge trio, Lightfoot, Westcott and Hort, to witness that whatever foes the Christians might be expected to fight and even to fear, they need never be afraid of truth.
(Ibid, p.83)

It is an impossible thing to diagnose the spirit of any age, to say what conditions its changing moods and temper, to say how much is owing to great thinkers and their books, how much to men of action, how much to the great impersonal forces which convulse political or economic structure, and how much to the coral-insect-like achievements of millions and millions of ordinary people.
(Ibid, p.83)

*   *   *

Going past the bookshop of a Protestant Truth Society the other day I was pulled up by a window empty of books but full of cards for St Valentine's Day. I wondered what their Puritan fathers would have thought of that: of course, it was not a decline into Popery but into modern tastelessness and commercialism, a far worse profanation of Christian ideals, the modern pagan year which joins Christmas, Valentine's Day, Fathers' Day and Mothers' Day in a mixture of sentimentalism and a commercial racket. And I remembered how those first Puritans rejected music and pictures and outward symbols from their churches and worship for the best of reasons, that such things had ceased to be media and had come between men and their God. And I thought of the drab and shoddy if harmless substitutes for Catholic symbolism which go on in our Free Church midst: from rose queens to totem poles, and of how we will allow any symbol on our communion tables except a cross.

48

I hope that our sons will have the courage in the name of that Christian liberty which was brought by the Reformers to join again what modern Protestantism has often parted asunder, the inward and the outward, the symbol and the meaning.
(*Manchester Guardian*, 4 February 1957)

After a spell in a Manchester hospital, Rupp reflects on the value of religious broadcasting for the housebound:
I remember switching over impatiently from a rather rarified experimental religious programme to 'Take It from Here' with a feeling of increased edification, since if the earthly house of our tabernacle has room for such wonderful creatures as Ron and Eth and Mr Glum, heaven must hold even more entrancing joys, while I thought (allow for my jaundiced mood) that hell might be a city much like the infinitely boring lower levels of religious dilettantism.
(Ibid, 16 September 1957)

The peril today is that Christians sink into a disgruntled, over-introspective mood. The Church may and ought to be 'under the Cross': it should never be 'the Church under the weather'.
(Ibid, 9 December 1957)

1958

It is part of the problem that on the other side of this Great Divide [between the Churches and the masses] the Churches have become introverted, preoccupied with problems of their own existence, own survival. Even the ecumenical movement itself represents a terrifying spiritual armaments bill.
    All the king's horses and all the king's men
    Couldn't put Humpty Dumpty together again.
What a waste that was! King's horses and king's men should have been riding away on the king's business. And the leaders of the Churches ought not to have to waste their energies in the delicate business of fumbling with broken ecclesiastical eggshells in long-drawn-out conversations about reunion; just as the local churches suffer from the wastage of resources resulting from our unhappy divisions.
(*Worldmanship and Churchmanship*, pp.10-11)

It is not so much talking as caring which is going to count, . . . people must know that we Christians are interested in them not as spiritual scalps to be hunted out but as comrades and friends who are

evidently valued for themselves and not as a means to an end . . . In the Church of Jesus Christ it is always 'washing day', the old humdrum, everlasting chores of doing God's own grubby, dirty business, wiping away tears and washing away sins. The importance of these things cannot be weighed or counted, for in the Kingdom of God to bring peace to one conscience may count more than a hundred religious meetings or a thousand ecumenical councils.
(Ibid, p.26)

[The Church] has great possessions. Through twenty centuries she has acquired a treasure house of truth, beauty and goodness, noble prayers, liturgies, poetry, buildings, works of art, the lives of the saints. The very hymn books of the Churches are witness that the Christians really have something to make a song about. Those outside the Church do not recognise these things or know their true worth. You do not need to be a Christian to admire the roof of King's College Chapel; and any teacher can make something of the poems of George Herbert or John Milton or the prose of John Bunyan. Yet there is something more. For the Church in the World is like Cinderella. She appears before men in the form of a servant, and only faith sees behind the rags those shining garments of a Bride adorned for her husband.[10] These other things, these gifts of the Church, are like the glass coach and the footmen which appear to the outsiders only as a rather drab affair of mice and pumpkin; and among these gifts, highest among them, are the comforts of the Gospel, those Christian perquisites so marvellously compressed in the words 'the means of grace and the hope of glory'. We Christians who know and enjoy these things need to remember that they were not given for us to enjoy alone, but we must share them with others. We must not grudge the wonders of the Father's house to our prodigal world.
(Ibid, p.28)

* * *

There seems to have been little remarkable about Luther's home or Luther's schooling. Between them his parents and his ushers knocked a good deal of sense into him, and nonsense out of him. Hans and Margaret Luther regarded their offspring with gruff pride, and he repaid them with something more than a customary filial piety. A certain

[10]   Cf p.86

directness, shrewdness and obstinacy mark his peasant background, and that fondness for proverbial wisdom, with which his writings are drenched. His home may have been superstitious and sombre, but his humour was bred there too.

('Luther and the German Reformation to 1529' in *The New Cambridge Modern History*, Vol. II, p.75)

Social unrest aggravated the tension in Saxony between reformers and radicals. There was nothing in Germany comparable with the English knights of the shire, gentlemen and burgesses, justices of the peace, who could take the strain at the middle levels of the social pyramid. Between the princes and the peasants were great inequalities and festering wrongs, while the machinery of amendment, cumbrous and often arbitrary, could ill keep pace with economic revolution. The Reformation itself had an undeniable effect on common men, with the stress upon a fundamental Christian equality before God, the assertion of a common Christian priesthood. That Storch the weaver should also be among the prophets might be as disconcerting to the Elector Frederick the Wise as the translation of his fellow craftsman, Bully Bottom, was to the Duke of Athens. But it was a sign of the times.

(Ibid, p.86)

* * *

I was interested to find that the Cambridge University Library (like most university libraries) does not take the *Mennonite Quarterly*, but does take *Men Only*. I can understand that it is the copyright law rather than a hidden but laudable levity on the part of the grave and reverend signors who direct these things, which is responsible for the inclusion of *Men Only* . . .

(*Manchester Guardian*, 6 January 1958)

Peter Breughel's great 'Procession to Calvary' . . . is his largest painting and to it he devoted great care. It is a busy, moving scene with scores of men and women journeying towards a distant place of execution where already two crosses are reared against the sky. There are two specially vivid scenes which draw all the attention towards them. On the one side there are the two thieves: nobody who has seen them with their chalk-white faces could ever forget them, or doubt that here Breughel shows us a real sixteenth-century execution. The other scene is the tremendous battle put up by the wife of Simon of Cyrene as she fights the soldiers who would impress her husband into a sordid act of mercy.

51

There is only one incident in the picture which receives no attention whatever. All the scores of frog-eyed spectators are looking everywhere but here: nobody notices at all, and we might easily miss in this picture the man who has fallen under the shadow of the Cross he is too weak to bear. 'Is it nothing to you, all ye that pass by?' And the cruel, rough picture suggests that the answer of history is, 'Nothing whatever!' So far from the Cross being the '(greatest drama ever staged' as Christians like to preach, it is purged even of drama. Here is not something to purge us with pity and terror, but something quite insignificant. But Breughel has something else to say. Here is plenty of religious emotion, but it is all misplaced. The friar and the priest hold crucifixes before the two thieves whom they would make repent. Upon Simon of Cyrene's chest there flutters a rosary and a crucifix. At the edge of the picture sit Mary, the Beloved disciple and the women – but in their ethereal drapery they are surely a caricature of all such groups from Botticelli to Durer. They are all in an ecstasy of emotion – but they are in the wrong place . . . The real place of execution is half a mile away. So even religion and religious devotion are drained away from the Cross itself . . . Only when you have seen these things do you notice one other fact. The figure 'under the Cross', stumbling in the ordure and the mire, is in the exact centre of the picture. In fact, all the lines find their focal point in him. So it is with the Cross in history, with the apparent irrelevance of God. To an age sated with Abelardian half-truth, Breughel brings the great godward objectivity of St. Anselm. The Cross bears God's meaning, not man's, not even religious, ecclesiastical man.
(Ibid, 31 March 1958)

The Church of England itself is on the edge of an experiment which should greatly extend its own lay representation. Indeed, Free Churchmen may well catch their breath at the suggestion that a House of Laity should come into being, able to meet by itself, for as Gilbert so nearly said:
　But then the prospect of a lot
　　Of Laity in close proximity
　All thinking by themselves, is what
　　No clergyman can face with equanimity.
And perhaps there has been nothing as daring since the first Elizabethan House of Commons! . . .
　Early Methodism was indeed a machine of wonderful flexibility, which the Holy Spirit could use as a silken glove. But in the nineteenth century it was pegged down with every building it put up, until it resembles today the famous picture of Gulliver pegged down on the

sand, unable to twist and turn. And since Methodist Union a written constitution, a tendency to trip over the manifold cables of its standing orders and a great bureaucratic machine have brought a rather alarming rigidity.
(Ibid, 26 May 1958)

If, in some distant post-Atomic Age, the poems of Lewis Carroll are rediscovered amid the debris of some vast European crater, scholars will no doubt decide that they contain very subtle theological allegories, and, at least as plausibly as they have thought to find an apocryphal Gospel among the Dead Sea Scrolls, the *Hunting of the Snark*, will be ingeniously discerned as an account of an important phase of the ancient Ecumenical Movement. The *Hunting of the Snark*, it will be remembered, is mainly an account of 'conversations' between members of a very mixed delegation. But from the beginning some members of that team are inhibited by depressing fears. The exhilarating quest for the Snark is offset for them by the fear that, too late, the Snark may turn out to be the dreaded Boojum, in which case they will 'softly and silently vanish away'. This has an evident parallel in present discussions about bishops, and in particular the distinction between the 'Historic Episcopate', about whose importance all Anglicans seem agreed, and a particular High Church doctrine of the 'Apostolic Succession'. And he who listens carefully for undertones in the various reports can easily discern the fear, not always expressed, of the non-Episcopal negotiators that they might enter into some reunion in which none are pledged to any particular interpretation of the episcopate only to find, too late, that the rigid 'catholic' doctrine has in fact triumphed and precious principles have vanished away. The historic Snark may prove to be the apostolic Boojum . . .

And if Christians cannot overcome their differences in the spirit of the gospel, it may be that the Lord of the Church will teach them by the Law, the hard way, the less excellent way also described in the *Hunting of the Snark*:

But the valley grew narrower and narrower still
And the evening got darker and colder,
Till (merely from nervousness, not from goodwill)
They marched along shoulder to shoulder.
(Ibid, 23 June 1958)

[The modern Methodist selection from the Psalms] has taken care to exclude everything in any way alarming or offensive. Here is no room for the cry in the dark, the stab in the back; the heartbroken desolation

53

amid the smoking ruins of a shattered sanctuary; the ugly bitterness of a mind pushed beyond endurance by unforgettable horrors . . .

In one of the most poignantly beautiful passages in all literature, the opening of Dante's *Purgatorio*, the poet hears on the morning breeze the song of those coming in to land upon the shore of a new world. 'In exitu Israel de Egypto' sang they all together with one voice. They have brought no luggage across the frontier of death, but they have brought with them their song. They did not learn those Psalms in the article of death, but as old soldiers banded together might sing 'Tipperary' or 'Lilli Marlene', so they come into a strange land singing one of the songs of Zion. Whatever else the Psalms may be, and whatever learned men may need to do with them, let them not forget their witness to the unity of the People of God, marching through Emmanuel's ground to fairer worlds on high.
(Ibid, 14 November 1958)

* * *

I cannot now argue about the policy of Jabez Bunting, whether he was a kind of Methodist Winston Churchill, or more like a Captain Bligh of the historic mutiny . . . If he took not so much Episcopacy as the Papacy into his system, he was a better Pope than most, and indeed I have little doubt that in that ecumenical history of the Church in several million volumes, which is being written in heaven by a committee of archangels it will be seen that Jabez Bunting can more than stand comparison as a statesman and as a Christian with the great Pius IX who was his near contemporary . . .

There was about him a wholeheartedness which I find abashing and moving. Methodist probationers probably take themselves more seriously than Methodist ministers at any other stage in their career, but it was more than pertness when ordinand Bunting replied to the question, 'Are you resolved to devote yourself wholly to God and His work?' with a simple, grave, 'I habitually do.' And when, in 1829, he apologised to Conference he said: 'I am sorry. I am not what I ought to be, but such as I am, I am body, soul and spirit a Methodist and a Methodist preacher, the grateful servant of Conference.' Let us remember him not for his frailties and mistakes, but as his congregations remembered him – a great preacher, who had an even greater gift of prayer, who would gather his people in his arms, and hold them up to supplication before the Living God.
('Our Fathers Who Begat Us', in *Methodist Recorder*, October 30, 1958)

* * *

54

As one grateful for the Protestant Reformation, I have not so learned Martin Luther as to place the quietness of mind of Christian people before obedience to the will of God.
('Church Relations', in *Methodist Recorder,* December 1958)

Perhaps, as one who spends much time thinking about the Reformation, I may register my conviction that there is nothing inherent in the 'historic episcopate' which violates the principles of Protestantism, least of all the 'Priesthood of All Believers'. No doubt clericalism and sacerdotalism are deadly evils. But in fact no form of Christian ministry is immune from them, and even laymen are susceptible of the virus, so that an anti-clerical local preacher might be just as wicked as an over-weening prelate, since both contradict that 'Form of a Servant' which is the one essential, the one fundamental ministry of Christ and His Church.
(Ibid)

* * *

One can ask whether any Protestant system which puts regeneration before justification (and that would go for Bucer, Calvin and their followers) has not missed an element of joy and wonder which Luther grasped but few Protestants (including Lutherans) after him.
(*Expository Times*, Vol. 69 p.273)

* * *

We need to remember what Professor Rowley has helped you to remember, that we belong to that one continuing People of God which stretches back into the mists of ancient history – we need to remember (tell it not in Manchester, whisper it not to Professor Rowley) that Old Testament studies ought properly to be regarded as a sub-department of Church History.
('The Importance of Denominational History' in *Baptist Quarterly*, July 1958, p.313)

There is the tendency to make the Anabaptists altogether too tidy, too respectable. Now if it is true, as Dr Payne says, that the Anabaptists produced more martyrs that all the other Protestant bodies, it is also true that they were associated with more genuine fanatics, more really wild men than any other body. They had some queer fellow-travellers, like

the Christian pacifists marching to Aldermaston or like the Underground movements in France and Greece at the end of the war, just because what they were doing was really revolutionary.
(Ibid, p.315)

I rejoice in these days that Dr Ernest Payne has become an ecclesiastical statesman, who knows that the making of history is even more important than writing it, but I sometimes grudge the fact that we have turned our most eminent Free Church historian into yet another ecumenical inter-continental missile.
(Ibid, p.317)

Our faith is something we share with the whole Church of Christ. Our history is something God has given us.
(Ibid, p.318)

1959

Like most academics, I rate highly a 'balanced' point of view. I have told myself, echoing South African friends, that men like Michael Scott and Trevor Huddleston are 'one-sided', and, on paper, I still think they are. But in the last days I have remembered staring at refugees in Berlin, along with Bishop Bell, and through the eyes of our conductor, Guy Clutton-Brock, and I can no longer treat world affairs as though I were marking one of my students' essays.
(*Manchester Guardian*, 3 April 1959)

On the postwar Kirchentag movement in the German Evangelical Church:
God is a wise schoolmaster who gives his children different lesson-books – to each Church perhaps its lesson-book. But there are times in Church history, and perhaps ours is one, when He says, 'You have looked at your book too long. You have got too used to the lesson. Change books! Read somebody else's!' So He tells the great State Churches to learn the lessons of freedom so hardly won by Free Churchmen long ago. And He tells Free Churchmen to listen to what in these days a great State Church has learned anew. The public witness of the Kirchentag has spread to France and Holland and Scotland. It makes some of us feel that it puts the Manchester 'Whit Walks' well back into the ecclesiastical museum where they belong.
(Ibid, 21 August 1958)

* * *

56

The story of Saul and the Witch of Endor is a reminder of the danger involved when we turn to the past in order to interpret the future. But the historian can do no other, even though to mingle history with prophecy is the hall-mark of the second-rate historian and the false prophet.
('The Future of the Methodist Tradition', in *London Quarterly & Holborn Review*, July 1959, p.264)

The oak tree and the mistletoe views of the Church . . . The radical reformers turned away from the oak tree of a Church with a continuous pedigree to the mistletoe of a truly believing People which consisted of isolated pockets of spiritual religion – in an idealized Primitive Church before the fall of Christianity in the second century or in the time of Constantine, in such medieval sects as could be plausibly reckoned as Reformers before the Reformation, and in themselves, the Anabaptists or the Puritans or the Methodist societies.
(Ibid, p.265)

* * *

Reformation Puritanism,[11] as well as Protestantism, began in Wittenberg. In the collision between Martin Luther and Andrew Karlstadt, we can discern the encounter between two complex patterns of reformation, and in the continuity and discontinuity between them a tension which has persisted through four centuries, and is still the biggest obstacle to those who seek to end the divisions among the variations of Protestantism.
('Andrew Karlstadt and Reformation Puritanism', in *The Journal of Theological Studies,* 1959, p.308[12])

Among the long line of witnesses against Karlstadt we must, it seems, include his wife. We must surely pity the man, but behind him we must see the young girl of sixteen, the roses dying from her cheeks as she strove to follow her unpredictable husband through all the

---

11 At the risk of adding to an overloaded vocabulary of typology, we use Puritanism in the Miltonic sense as a movement for 'the reform of Reformation itself'. [E.G.R.]
12 See also *Patterns of Reformation* (1969) Part II in which much of this article is incorporated.

57

changes and chances of his vulnerable life, eternally traipsing the long roads, in rain and snow, up hill and down dale, until when he died she was a helpless cripple, an old woman at forty, confined to bed with arthritis and the stone, writing a terrible lament to Luther whose heart turned over that a wife could so write about her Christian husband.

[Luther] made the Protestant church safe for the music of John Sebastian Bach, and for that greatest son of the Saale valley, George Frederick Handel. Those of us who, with Martin Luther and Richard Hooker, are Protestant but not Puritan can still turn gratefully to Luther's profound rationale in seeking to combat the petrifying moralism into which Protestantism so dangerously falls, in defying that sectarianism which imperils the return to Christian unity.
(Ibid, pp.325-6; *Patterns of Reformation*, pp.151-3)

* * *

Show me a parson's library and I will tell you something, though not perhaps the all-important thing, about his ministry. The man who stopped reading when he left college; the man (you can date it on his shelves!) caught in a crisis of conscience between his inclinations and the demands of his pastoral ministry; the man who has kept up his reading at all costs and for whom his books have been a lifetime's illumination and refreshment. A library (some of us learnt it in the blitz) is an intimation of mortality. In a few years what we have painfully gathered will be scattered among the second-hand bookshops and jumble sale stalls. 'These things shall vanish all; the City of God remaineth.' And truth is the shining bulwark of that city.
(*Manchester Guardian*, 16 October 1959)

1960

Some older writers exaggerated the influence of Bucer and the other foreign refugee scholars, Peter Martyr and John a Lasco, on the English Prayer Books and on Archbishop Cranmer's theology of the eucharist. Recently Dr Dugdale has been concerned to show that Cranmer and Ridley had minds of their own and had read the 'old Fathers' on their own account. But perhaps he does not do justice to the immense experience of these exiles in this matter. Imagine the captain of a village cricket team who discovered on the eve of the great match with Little Snodgrass that Lock and Laker and Trueman were staying in the village. Would he not seek their advice about 'how to get the beggars out'? Would he not, if he could, smuggle them into his team disguised

as the baker's second cousin and the undertaker's nephew and the new assistant curate? And remember, Martin Bucer was the greatest ecclesiastical spin bowler of the age, the very model of a modern ecumenical.
(*Protestant Catholicity*, pp.23-4)

The meaning of Reformation studies is that the Church is not *Ecclesia Reformata*, as reformed once for all and needing never to be purged again, but *Ecclesia Reformanda*, always in reformation, always under the present, living, active role of Christ Himself, speaking by his Word, guiding by his Spirit, as it was in the beginning, is now, and ever shall be, world without end.
(Ibid, p.32)

* * *

Protestantism is more sensitive to the spirit of each age, easily succumbs to pressures of history, against which Rome has grown an extra skin. But it is also more open to new truths emerging in history itself. And one must ask whether canons of 'catholic tradition' derived from the patristic age are not derived from a thought world on the one hand too insulated and introverted, and on the other hand more influenced by secular influences than orthodoxy can easily admit; one would press these questions in relation to the ministry, to the place of women and the laity in the Church, and of the modern concepts of democracy. It is one thing to say that the Church ought not to accommodate its faith to the spirit of the age, must not come to terms with secular thought on the world's terms; it is another to behave as though the Church had nothing to learn, nothing to re-think, nothing to discard after its encounters with great movements of the human spirit. Surely a sensitiveness toward such possibilities is a mark of catholicity.
(Ibid, pp.51-2)

A few years ago an article in the *Architectural Review* gave the world the grim new word 'Subtopia'. It showed the drab uniformity of our urban civilization, the roads and road signs, the petrol pumps and concrete lamp standards, the town centres almost identical in any suburb of San Francisco, New York, Johannesburg, London, Berlin, Tokyo. Are we not creating a kind of religious subtopia – a suburban moralistic mediocrity of thought and experience and behaviour, a pattern of Nonconformity which varies very little from Atlanta, Georgia to Port Elizabeth and Salisbury and London, which fails in a crisis to produce heroic witness, . . . not at the level of official pronouncements,

but in the quality of the average Church member? What has happened to that discipline which was once our glory?
(Ibid, pp.53-4)

* * *

We have learned a great deal of child psychology. We have forgotten the truth of old Thomas Fuller, that children's clothes should be made a size larger than life, that they may have something to grow into.
(*Manchester Guardian*, 12 February 1960)

All the teaching of Jesus about the birds, the lilies of the field, the grass, and reposeful trust in God which, as Pascal said, we might almost mistake for the naivete of a simpleton, is the teaching of him who agonised with his temptations in the burning desert at the beginning of his ministry, and in the not less cruel coolness of a garden at its end. There is, it seems, an ambivalence between temptation and trust, and the heights and depths of confidence in God come only to those who take seriously their Christian warfare, who wage the good fight of faith to the point of death: death which, for them, is swallowed up in victory.
(Ibid, 11 March 1960)

Some years ago, safely locked and barred in for the night in an Oxford college, I heard somebody being attacked in the lane outside and shall never forget the bloodcurdling sound of the desperate, repeated cry, 'Help! Help!' . . . It would be well for us, safely locked and barred in our Christian world of dear proprieties, if we could listen to noise from outside and take up our newspapers, remembering how all around us, all the time, there are men and women in such dire distress of mind, body and estate that it is almost beyond coherent articulation. They speak for humanity, for those depths of the human heart which we visit seldom, and where we stay no longer than we must, but where we know our need: we are at odds with life, and sore let and hindered from finding our immortal destiny.
(Ibid, 16 December 1960)

* * *

When I first visited the German Methodists after the war, I was, to be frank, a little patronising. Against the resistance of the Confessing Church, against the massive Lutheran tradition, was this not a rather old-fashioned, pietistic sect? But I came, I saw, and not once or twice, and almost against my will, my mental rearguard actions have been beaten down. And now I will confess – here in a German setting, with

60

its own historic tradition, is authentic Methodism, scriptural holiness spread through the length and breadth of a sombre land, shining the more joyfully in contrast, but abounding in hope and in the fruits of the Spirit.
(*Methodist Recorder*, 22 September 1960)

1961

The Reformation of the sixteenth century was, among other things, an explosion. It is as though some great ship, going on its lawful occasions, had been suddenly stopped by some disastrous upheaval – its occupants suddenly plunged into a situation of crisis, called to make desperate improvisations, where men and women found their values forming into perspectives which they would never have found but for this dire emergency. Thomas More and Hugh Latimer knew what it was to 'stand upon life or death'. Out of that emergency came the drastic changes about which men had talked in vain for centuries, the reform of the Church in head and members, and these emerged as the patterns of Protestantism and the Counter-Reformation.
('Reformation and Unity', an address given in Cambridge during the Octave of Prayer for Christian Unity; in *The Modern Churchman*, Vol. IV, p.182)

So far [in the Anglican-Methodist conversations] no suggestions have been made which would involve the Church of England in any drastic upheaval. They stand foursquare upon the Lambeth Quadrilateral: you may go about her and admire those bulwarks – how easy it would be in such a situation for Anglicans to feel:
> Leave them alone
> And they'll come home
> Wagging their tails behind them!

For Anglicans nothing much more is involved than the uncomfortable business of squeezing up in a railway carriage to admit newcomers – it is a bother, but by the time the luggage has been rearranged and everybody has reseated themselves as near their original position as possible, we are prepared to sit by one another in peace and good temper. But for the Methodists, it is to be much more like having to walk out of an underground train with their luggage and then walk along the dark tunnel – not knowing whether the live rail has been switched off or not.
(Ibid, p.183)

Sometimes some Methodists are accused of a 'deep, dark plot to hand Methodism over to the Church of England'. Occasionally I wish such a plot existed: sometimes I even wish I could join such a plot! ... Would that there were among us those who could qualify as 'the Plotters' – with the exuberant courage of a Guy Fawkes, the eloquence of a Mirabeau or Danton, even the inventiveness of a Titus Oates! Would that we could envisage groups of ardent longers for reunion sitting up into the small hours, resolving schemes and difficulties, but deeply concerned and personally utterly committed to a great enterprise. But there is a more excellent way. It is first the way of charity. For we have to convince our fellow-Christians, and convert them: we cannot browbeat them into reunion, and this is the one conversation we can jeopardize not so much by what we say as the way we say it. How many of us simply evoke sales resistance by putting a great case badly. But most excellent of all will it be to offset the opposition not by something deep and dark, but by something clear and high – not a plot but a vision – a vision of a Church truly evangelical and catholic, dedicated and renewed, going about its Master's business, showing a place of healing and unity to a broken and divided world. This is the way forward. May we be like those shepherds on the Delectable Mountains – through whose perspective glass others may turn towards Mount Zion, and whose hands like ours will tremble to see 'something like a gate, and also something of the glory of the place'.
(Ibid, pp.184-5)

* * *

Human speech is a sacrament: it is at the root of all human life and we do not ponder enough the mystery whereby words pass from one human mind to another, bringing communion between men and nations. Marvellous too is the way in which words, as tools, come out of the changing life of men. Sometimes theologians show how the elements of the bread and wine in the eucharist symbolise human existence and make them a symbolic offering of all our life. The English Bible should be similarly regarded: here are words of men, wrought out of everyday existence in the world. And in the Bible they are found fully framed together into a holy temple for the Living Word of God, breaking out in life and truth to the farthest range of the creation and the deepest recesses of the human heart.
(*Manchester Guardian*, 13 January 1961)

The modern 'eminent historian' is a recognizable type. He finished
with documents and records at the Ph.D. stage and proceeded to
develop an Autolycan flair for snapping up the results of other people's
theses, which he describes in a style sufficiently readable and indeed
elegant to pass muster for great historical writing. Tiring as these
enfants terribles may be to colleagues unenamoured with verbal
Technicolor, they are in much popular demand on the wireless and
elsewhere and move inexorably towards their destined knighthood.
(Ibid, 10 March 1961)

No doubt when Church historians look back on 1961 it will be
apparent that the craze for 'Bingo' outside the Churches and the
concern for Christian Stewardship within were both marks of an
affluent society (together with the Decline and Fall of the Jumble
Sale) . . . It is hard to say who have done more harm in the Church:
worldly Christians or those who have not been worldly enough. There
is much in the New Testament to suggest that religious people have a
lot to learn from those who pursue this world's goods with expertise,
and even from those unjust stewards like the cynic who said that to
serve God and Mammon is like all worthwhile things very difficult. For
the flourishing church, we know, all things work for financial good; but
from the declining church that which it has is taken away . . .
An affluent church in an affluent society – I hear a warning bell
somewhere. I remember that the Protestant Reformation was sparked
off by a highly successful Stewardship campaign (called indulgences,
but using high-flown language not dissimilar from what is now
available) . . . Let us remember that some of our churches need as
desperately a new technique of prayer and devotion.
(Ibid, 2 June 1961)

. . . 'the old Ecumenical gang' – that travelling circus of Top
Ecclesiastical People which got on the move at Amsterdam in 1948 and
which will soon, with but little alteration, converge on New Delhi,
admirable people all, but perhaps slow to believe that God could raise
children to Abraham from much stonier soil.
(Ibid, 30 June 1961)

If the scientist's is the presumptuous sin of ancient alchemy, the
historian's is the sin of witchcraft. Out of materials as heterogeneous
and oddly assorted (records, letters, diaries) as the witches' cauldron in
Macbeth he brews his potion. He summons spirits from the vasty deep,
and they do come, though what relation they bear to the flesh and blood

who lived and died is still the grand, unanswered question from the days when Saul summoned Samuel at Endor.
(Ibid, 22 September 1961)

A member of the Women's Bright Hour who really offers her cancer or arthritis to God as doing more for the Kingdom than all our great confabulations . . .
(Ibid, 17 November 1961)

1962

There are in this play [*Luther* by John Osborne] fine insights, great obtuseness. It shows us Luther's doubts, his scepticism, his anguish, but little of his joy and confidence and boldness – which could cry out, 'We know Satan's Devices, but they are as nothing compared with the Devices of God.' We feel his perfect hatred for God's enemies as he conceived them, but nothing of his deep compassion; his melancholy, but not his giant humour. We see the real introverted, lonely figure, and miss his friends – and he had many; his charm, which could soothe the savage breast of a hostile papal official; the way in which as the years went by he gathered, like Napoleon, his marshals round him: Melanchthon, Jonas, Bugenhagen. We see the rebel, we miss the leader – whose example and words put heart into multitudes . . .
('John Osborne and the Historical Luther', a lecture delivered at the University of Aberdeen, October 1961; in *The Expository Times*, February 1962, p.151[13])

* * *

This commentary [Luther's lectures on *Hebrews* delivered in 1517-18] gains in interest, too, because of what was happening outside the lecture room. The great church struggle had begun with Luther's ninety-five Theses against Indulgences at the end of 1517, and the months when these lectures were given were for Luther a lonely, anxious time. Many of his friends were scared, and at this time a deputation of his fellow monks begged him not to bring disgrace on their order. He had to break off the lectures to attend the Chapter of the

---

13 An expanded version of this lecture appeared in the *Cambridge Quarterly*, Winter 1965-66, pp.28-42.

Augustinian Order at Heidelberg in the spring of 1518. Our manuscript breaks off in the middle of chapter eleven, that great roll call, the battle honours of the Old Testament pioneers of faith. It may be accidental that the manuscript does stop at this point. But how appropriate it was! Luther's students must have wondered what would happen to their professor – would he stay in Wittenberg, perhaps to be arrested or even burned? Or would he run away – perhaps to France or Bohemia? And so, that morning when Luther stopped at the place where Moses, having slain the Egyptian, had to run for his life – 'And so he had to flee – into Midian' – I dare say the sleepiest pair of eyes widened at that wonderful exit line, as in a hush the burly figure stepped down, passed through the door, and they heard the echo of his footsteps die away.

There is a saying of Earl Haig to which I often turn: 'No news is either as good or as bad as it seems when you first hear it.' That is true not only in life but in historical scholarship. Historians live by reassessment and revaluing. They are always sifting old judgments in the light of new evidence. Almost every day some historian or other claims to have revised the estimate of this or that historical person, this or that battle, this or that treaty, this or that century and epoch.

In the end, things settle down and what was thought to be an exclamation mark on the page of history turns out to be, after all, just a comma, or even a speck of dust to be blown off.

('Young Professor Luther', *The Listener*, October 18, 1962)

* * *

During this year of Grace, 1962, while his Free Church and Anglican colleagues have publicly extolled the virtues of the 1662 Prayer Book or the heroism of the Ejected Clergy, a Methodist has felt rather like the Irishman who wistfully inquired, 'Is this a private fight, or can anyone join in?'

('Clerical Integrity – 1662' in *The Expository Times*, February, 1963, p.145)

Among the more obvious reasons for the breakdown of negotiations 1660-62 was the fact that on both sides memories could not be forgotten or forgiven and, as in our own day, good men were glad to be able to find high-sounding reasons to excuse shabby actions. Throughout Church History there has been a constant alliance between cruelty and honest fear.

(Ibid, p.146)

After a century most religious movements begin to wear thin. The Puritans were not what they had been in their beginning – their leaders were no longer angry young men with fire in their bellies – like Penry, Greenwood, Barrow – but milder, middle-aged men who had to take care of their stomachs. They had no longer the wit or the ruthlessness which under the First Elizabeth had engineered a formidable resistance movement, skilfully and almost successfully organized. Perhaps, above all, the great Puritan mind was tired . . . I do not want to exaggerate this tiredness, but I think there are signs that the Nonconformists, called to take their stand 'under the Cross' in 1662, had to evoke heroism out of attenuated resources, rather like those in Germany who, in 1933, heroically became the 'Confessing Church'.
(Ibid, p.146

The angry seventeenth-century debate between Samuel Walker and Edmund Calamy, comparing the sufferings of the Church of England men with those of the Dissenters has something of the dignity of warriors comparing honourable scars, and in comparison with them the pedantic fuss over statistics by modern academics has more the air of old ladies comparing operations.
(Ibid, pp.146-7)

To be exiles abroad was the pain of the Pilgrim Fathers. To be exiled at home, the deadlier hurt of the Nonconformists . . . Somewhere here is the deepest hurt with which in three centuries Nonconformists have been wounded in the house of their friends. It is not the loss of worldly rights or civil dues, not the spite and petty persecution in little places by little men, to which too often we have replied in sectarian kind – but that we have been by implication excluded from that pure and reformed part of Christ's Church in this country, our integrity questioned in the deepest, surest part of our conscience, awareness of the promises of God, and of the grace and presence of our Lord. This most sharply comes home at the point of pastoral care. For this crisis was a crisis of the pastoral office . . . And while we sympathize with Catholics trying to adjust an ancient theology of Grace and of the Ministry, to those facts which the Ecumenical encounter now make inescapable, we must abide by our conviction that there are not varying levels of grace but only the Grace of our Lord Jesus Christ, and there are not ministries, some more or some less authentic, but one ministry, His who bears the form of a Servant.
(Ibid, p.147)

I spoke of a crisis of conscience . . . Whether we are Anglicans who commemorate the Prayer Book, or whether we remember the Great Ejectment, we must all stand in penitence: penitence that, in the crisis of European conscience, Christian men were engrossed in their own churchly existence, squabbling about liturgies and theologies, while the common people of England went their own desperate way through the profligate decades of Restoration England – to which the Church belatedly turned with the palliatives of the Society for the Reformation of Manners, and a renewed zeal for philanthropy, no longer as the English Church, but instead as a set of rival denominations from which in time the mass of the nation would be more and growingly estranged. (Ibid, p.148)

* * *

In 1544 a British army of some 40,000 men was in Flanders, and not for the first or last time got itself bogged down almost within sight of the white cliffs of Dover . . . The expedition began at Calais, and succeeded only in capturing Boulogne, and having made the British Empire safe for day excursions without passports, the troops relaxed and watched the naval goings-on in the Channel, the highlight of which was the capsizing of our new flagship, the *Mary Rose,* through sheer naval incompetence, while the French sailed up the Solent. ('John Bradford, Martyr', a sermon preached in Manchester Cathedral, 1 July 1962, in *London Quarterly and Holborn Review,* 1963, p.50)

I remember in October 1945 driving with Bishop Bell through the suburbs of Berlin to the grim, red brick fortress of Tegel, where his friend Dietrich Bonhoeffer had spent the last weeks of his life before being taken away to be shot by the Nazis, and the stories men were telling of Bonhoeffer's influence on his guards, and how he had written letters and meditations which would one day be published. (Ibid, p.54)

* * *

The image of priesthood in ecumenical discussions about the ministry is often calamitously abstract – like the glossy catalogues of clerical outfitters . . . with their pictures of amiable clerical zombies variously garbed in Catholic copes or Protestant pullovers, from birettas to Holy Joes. But the true shepherds of the flock of Christ are men, known to their friends as Tom, Dick, or maybe as Harry. (*Manchester Guardian,* 12 January 1962)

What is now called 'corporate thinking' has great merits, but too often its results are dehydrated committee-English, a kind of 'instant theology', tiresome and unprepossessing . . . There was a time when the Ecumenical Movement needed the profundities of Professor Karl Barth. Just now it stands in still greater need of the clarities of Miss Enid Blyton.
(Ibid, 31 August 1962)

1963

Is there not something slightly ridiculous in attempting to plug the 225th anniversary of the Conversion of John Wesley, if not rather ominous in a Church which ignores Ascension Day, and allows Trinity Sunday to be submerged by Sunday School anniversaries without turning a hair? Our modern Methodist calendar is coming to resemble those cricket matches where at every ball, some new record has to be applauded:

> There was a young curate of Dover
> Who bowled twenty wides in one over,
>> Which had never been done
>> By a clergyman's son
> On a Wednesday, in August, in Dover.

This overloading of the Christian Year was one of the signs that medieval religion had run to seed, but at least the gimmicks were always subordinate to the person, her wheel to St Catherine, her beard to St Uncumber. I have always distrusted the sentimental anatomizing of the Popish cult of the 'Sacred Heart of Jesus', but I confess that a cult of the Warmed Heart of John Wesley would be even more lamentable.
('Honest to Wesley', in *Methodist Recorder*, 13 June, 1963)

* * *

'The Voice of Methodism' – Friend, I thank thee for this noble phrase! But how shall a man discern it? It is timely to remember the witty comment on the poetry of William Wordsworth: 'Two voices are there – one is of the deep. The other, of an old, half-witted sheep'! . . . Just now let us rejoice that we have heard the authentic voice of our dear Mother in the election by the South African Conference of the Rev S. M. Mokitimi as President; a splendid gesture, courageous, and it may be costly, but one by reason of which all Methodists across the world can hold their heads a little higher and hard-pressed Christians in the Rhodesias and the Deep South, and it may be in Nottingham and

Notting Hill, can take heart. For if, as a Church, we compromise here, we relapse into a world sect, and our needful protests against booze and bingo and the like become futile bleatings indeed.
(*Methodist Recorder*, 12 December, 1963)

1964

It makes a difference to what we do with our lives here and now whether we have to budget for this world, or for an eternal destiny.
(*Last Things First*, p.7)

Even in those countries professing the materialism of Karl Marx there is an adherence to moral values, an appeal to loyalty and patriotism, a drab Puritanism indeed of intense moral earnestness, and a capacity for righteous indignation about the shortcoming of others which recalls the Nonconformist conscience when it runs to seed.
(Ibid, p.9)

The Church is not simply a means to an end, to improving the world and answering its questions. We often do think of the Church in this way, as though it were a kind of oracle. And if you treat the Church like a slot-machine, you get a slotty answer; the stereotyped, platitudinous cards telling your fortune which come out of a weighing machine are like many of the resolutions of ecclesiastical assemblies about current affairs. If you want to know the nature of the Church, you must not look at the point where it is most closely connected with its cultural environment.
(Ibid, p.13)

To learn loyalty to a real community is not easy. It brings our Christian profession down to earth. Sometimes the discipline of worshipping in drab, out-of-date buildings, with unattractive ornaments and second-rate music, may be real indeed. You remember how Brer Rabbit came to rejoice that he was born and bred 'in dat Old Briar Patch', because in this way he learned how to cope with thorns in later life. Sometimes there may even be something of a cross in this loyalty to little people in little buildings, yet that local church is for us a gate of heaven.
(Ibid, p.18)

C. S. Lewis makes a valiant attempt to square Adam with history in his *Preface to Paradise Lost*, and to think of the first man as a

primitive, animal-like being, who yet in his simple goodness would be far our superior. But the result is a kind of theological Winnie the Pooh with a halo[14], or Mole in *Wind in the Willows*.
(Ibid, p.24)

[Total depravity] is total in the sense of being entire. No part of human life is exempt from it. Just as you can't say, 'I am ill – most of me has influenza, but my right elbow is quite well, thank you,' so we cannot say, 'Ah, man's reason, that's all right, so that the eggheads and boffins will get us out of it' – when in fact they simply invent bigger and better bombs. Nor can you isolate one part of humanity – say the Nordic race – or the democracies – or the working classes – or religious people – not even a coming generation of 'mature Christians' and say: these are the heroes of the piece.
(Ibid, p.25)

Conscience is not infallible. It is like a watch which goes wrong if it is not kept in trim, if it is not constantly re-wound, if it is not constantly checked by some outside standard. But we ignore it at our peril – and sometimes if we listen to it and will not or cannot do anything about it, we can build ourselves a prison and a little hell on earth. For most people that doesn't happen. For one thing we have an endless capacity for fooling ourselves. Man is by definition an excuse-making animal. You remember the end of Book IX of *Paradise Lost* – that day which began with a lovers' tiff and ended with a downright row – with a world lost somewhere in between:

> Thus they in mutual accusation spent
> The fruitless hours, but neither self-condemning,
> And of their vain contest appeared no end.

And then, as Augustine says, we glamorize evil, we never see it as mean and ugly and squalid, but find high-sounding words for it. You remember the lady in *Trial by Jury* – 'she may very well pass for 43, in the dusk, with the light behind her'. That is how we see our besetting sins, in the dusk, with the light behind them – artificial light.
(Ibid, p.27)

That the holy God receives sinners, that here and now I may have fellowship with God, is the paradox within which is the joy and wonder of the Christian religion. Sometimes Christians have dared not believe

---

[14] An echo of an article in the *Methodist Recorder* as far back as 23 June 1949

it. They have spoken of free forgiveness but of temporal penalties which remain, for which men must make satisfaction. But that is as though the father in the parable had said: 'Bring forth the best robe and put it on him; but remember that it has to go back to Moss Brothers after the week-end; and get out the second best sackcloth for him to eat with the cold fatted calf on Monday morning.'
(Ibid, p.30)

In October 1945, in an Upper Room in the shattered city of Stuttgart, some leaders of the German Evangelical Church stood face to face for the first time since the war began with representatives of the World Council of Churches from the allied countries, Holland, France, America and Britain. It was a tense and difficult moment, badly needing a gesture of some kind. The Germans had all been brave leaders of their church, most of them had been in prison. Then Martin Niemoller handed round a document they had prepared, one of the few prophetic Christian utterances of our time, which has become known as the Stuttgart Declaration. In it they said:
> We acknowledge ourselves to be bound together with
> our German people not only in a solidarity of suffering,
> but also in a solidarity of guilt – we accuse ourselves . . .
Corporate guilt and corporate penitence are difficult conceptions, but they are important. In so far as the Church is 'in Christ' she is identified with men, taking also the form of a Servant and, in compassion, in deed and in word, sharing all the life of the world and bringing it all into relation with Jesus Christ, in the solidarity of his High Priestly intercession. Yet profound and intimate as is the union between Christ and his Church, we must never blur the distinction between him and it, between what he has done once for all, perfectly and sufficiently, and what we do for and in communion with him.
(Ibid, pp.32-3)

Let us . . . admit that one version of the Apostles' Creed reads: 'The resurrection of *this* body' and that until well into the eighteenth century most Christians believed that it was this identical physical body which would be raised again at the last day. That brought problems, of course. Even the early Fathers were worried about sailors who got eaten by fish, which fish got eaten by other sailors, who got eaten by more fish, and so on, as to how it would all be sorted out, the fatal dilemma of 'Ilkla Moor 'baht Hat' –
> Then worms'll coom and eat thee oop,
> Then dooks'll coom and eat oop worms,
> Then us'll coom and eat oop dooks . . .

Put this doctrine in a modern setting – Stanley Spencer's great painting, 'Resurrection in Port Glasgow' – and it is quite intolerable to modern Christians. But Spencer drives home a truth too. Like the other two great visions of heaven, in Dante and Bunyan, his vision is well and truly earthed . . . At least he reminds us that heaven is not some cloud-cuckoo-land which only poets can imagine and philosophers enjoy. His people are not at all religious types; rather they are jolly sailor men and barmaids and not a bit highbrow. They would be as lost in Dean Inge's Kingdom of Absolute Values as he would have been queuing with them for fish and chips. Here is the apotheosis of the ordinary people, like the obituary which appeared in a newspaper a few years ago:

The trumpet sounds, Peter cries come
The pearly gates open, and in walks Mum.
(Ibid, pp.39-40)

. . . the well-known manner of some preachers of looking a difficulty straight between the eyes and then walking as quickly as possible by on the other side.
(Ibid, p.41)

Just as the individual Christian has much to learn from the psychologist, so the Christian Church has much to learn from the sociologist, to accept the implications of a religion of incarnation, the most materialist of all the great religions. This means recognizing the extent to which it is conditioned like any other community by the pressures of history. The tradition of the Church may be a kind of Gulf Stream which warms and affects the direction of the other currents in the surrounding ocean of history, but it is in turn affected also by the wider stream of human life in which it lives and moves. Somewhere here is a whole doctrine of Christian missions, for the Christian gospel is always rooted in a body, in the culture in which it is set.
(Ibid, p.44)

There are those today who believe that organized Christianity is so sick that, in Dietrich Bonhoeffer's phrase, they hope for the coming of a 'religionless Christianity'. They have a grave and serious point. An introverted Christendom has become isolated and insulated from modern man. An Augustinian pietism has so developed the doctrine of sin as to forget the true humanism of the gospel. The Church can no longer say, 'Mirror, mirror on the wall, which is the true community of us all?', and see its own reflection as the answer in a world where men and women out of the heights and depths of human joy and pain, and the hard and desperate business of achieving political freedom and economic equality, have in fact seen and experienced deeper truths than the Christian experience can express.

Yet surely the idea of abandoning the Church must have occurred to God long ago? . . . For there have been times in church history when things were even more shameful and disastrous: in the tenth century when the Church was headed by a 'pornocracy'; and in the late fifteenth century when the great religious orders were as salt which has lost its savour; or like parts of the Church of England in the eighteenth and nineteenth centuries, which provoked Arnold's famous 'The Church of England . . . who can save?'; or the French Church when it provoked the terrible reaction, 'ecrasez l'infame'. Dare we ever forget that the Church is the People of God, chosen not for its efficiency or its gifts, but out of the divine pity? 'How shall I give thee up, O Ephraim?' (Ibid, p.46)

We may wonder whether Dante's Hell poses any more acute problem for believers than this real, present world . . . Most of us Christians live in a fairly protected kind of world. The world of violence and hostility, of law courts and police and prisons and executions – and beyond, of torture and concentration camps and secret police – touches us not at all. We never really square these things with our thought of God. And I wonder what would be the result of a card-vote among Christians whether there is a place for retributive punishment in our legal system, and therefore presumably in the universe?
It is when we move from Dante up to Dante's God that the trouble comes. On strict justice, on the level of Shylock and his pound of flesh, nobody in Dante's Hell can complain – nor could we. If to make the punishment fit the crime be the mark of a humane Mikado, then a more humane Mikado than Dante's God never did exist. He may be like the headmaster who was described as 'a beast – but a just beast'. The trouble is that a God who is compounded of Shylock, the Mikado and Dr Busby of Westminster doesn't add up to the God and Father of our Lord Jesus Christ.
(Ibid, pp.50-1)

To some of us to unsettle the minds of theological students is the object all sublime of all our instruction, though unlike the Mikado most of us never hope to achieve it.
(Ibid, p.53)

73

The world of the New Testament is a world of heights and depths, of mountains of joyful vision and precipices and crevasses of terrifying danger, so different from the smooth and rounded mediocrity of our religious Sub-topias.
(Ibid, p. 57)

Not long ago at a service I was inveigled into allowing the anthem to come right at the end, after my sermon. It proved to be Keble's 'Sun of my soul . . .', a long-ish hymn, but made even longer by an ingenious contrivance whereby the bass and tenors repeated everything three bars after the sopranos and altos – so that in the end I brooded bitterly over the last words:
> Till in the ocean of thy love
> We lose ourselves in heaven above . . .
Can you imagine a worse predicament than to be lost in the middle of an ocean – feebly calling 'Mayday! Mayday!' to an unheeding universe? Or to be lost in heaven – of all places; in that vast Messianic banquet to find the tables spread and ourselves the only one who had no place with a name beside it – lost in heaven? O Paradise were wilderness enow! Surely a better image is to say that we *find* ourselves in heaven above, because when we are face to face with the Beatific Vision of God himself, Father, Son and Holy Spirit, we have come home, have found our place and are most truly and finally ourselves.
(Ibid, pp.58-9)

* * *

From a comprehensive and trenchant critique of an evangelical Anglican 'Consideration' of the Anglican-Methodist Report:

Dr Packer and his friends are better at laying down the law than the gospel, and nothing is more depressing than their willingness to write off any appeal to the grace of God as mere verbiage, ecumenical good manners, or even theological agnosticism. Methodists have not so learned their Bible or their Charles Wesley.
(*Consideration Re-considered: an examination of 'The Church of England and the Methodist Church*, p.12)

For two thousand years the world has gone its way, with a Christian church in its midst. In that time men have learned a myriad of truths, some inspiring in joy, some terrible in wrath: truths learned out of the tumults of the nations, the visions of seers and artists and poets: the discoveries of science: the experiences of pity and terror of the vast

masses on mankind. Has God nothing to do then with all this? Is this nothing to do with Christ? Are we to think of the Church as isolated and insulated from it all? As the Church ponders the Holy Scriptures, is there no help, no guidance from the Holy Spirit in relating the one gospel, the apostolic testimony, to each new epoch? Is it not in the end the one fatal derogation from the authority of Holy Scripture, and from the reverence due to the Holy Spirit, to restrict them to an introverted religious pietism? Somewhere here is the failure of nerve which is the real betrayal of fundamentalism.
(Ibid, pp.18-19)

There follows a comparison between Methodist and Anglican polities . . . [The Rev. Colin Brown] contrasts painful autocracies of Methodism with the liberties of the Church of England. What touches him on the raw (for he refers to it twice in half a page) is the fact that the Methodist Conference tells its candidates what theological college they must attend. The grisly picture is conjured up of nervous theological students being hi-jacked by tough tutorial bodyguards, and bundled off blindfold in taxis to Wesley House, Cambridge, or Didsbury College, Bristol, into a sadly regimented world which knows not the Liberty Hall conditions of Mirfield or of Clifton. The seriousness of the point is that it reveals the complete ignorance of Mr Brown of the Methodist view of ministerial training, the fact that the whole Church accepts financial responsibility for the training of its accepted candidates, and that the teaching staff of Methodist colleges represents the whole Church [so that they] are not seminaries of this or that theological or ecclesiastical party.
(Ibid, pp.46-7)

I would put to them a question – If you can live in the same household of faith with Anglo-Catholics, how can you deny to Methodists the same possibility? If you regard the Anglo-Catholics as in vital, grievous error, how can you stay in the same Church without being guilty, in Dr Kingsley Barrett's hard words, of doctrinal levity or weakness? How can you abide with them without a crisis of conscience of the kind which drove the Nonconformists and the Non-Jurors into the wilderness? But if you so abide because fundamentally there is a deeper unity, of grace and faith and loyalty to the one Lord of the one Church, then how can you forbid Methodists to come inside too, and live with them?
(Ibid, pp.57-8)

* * *

75

Under the title 'Requiem for a Dead City' Rupp described the
carnage and mass destruction of the Allied raid on Dresden on the
night of 13 February, 1945, after which there were over 35,000
identified casualties:

How shall we keep Lent? Reading nice little devotional books,
enjoying our Palm Sunday cantata, becoming emotionally moved by the
story of the Passion? Or must we not, somehow, remember that the Son
of Man still bows under his Cross, staggers and falls in the least of
these, his brethren? And ought not ours to be the deep penitence which
seeks somewhere, somehow, to share his costly suffering?
(*Methodist Recorder*, 12 March, 1964)

* * *

Elizabeth I of England had the long Tudor nose for rebels, and she
had reason to sniff at Master Calvin. For wherever his notions went,
there was a menace for despots. So far from belief in predestination
breeding an enervating fatalism, it rather engendered a robust taste for
liberty, a race of free men, a crop of free institutions in one country after
another, in Holland, Scotland, France, and in the New World.
('Calvin, Prophet of Christian Order', in *The Times*, 27 May 1964)

* * *

The sub-conscious sometimes makes shrewd comments and as I
went into the Faith and Order Conference at Nottingham I caught
myself humming 'great argument, but evermore came out by that same
door wherein I went'. And yet, five days later when I left by those
same portals, It was humming the Te Deum.

It did not begin too well, with ecumenical platitudes familiar
enough. And then, the Church of England, the mother of us all, on the
first Sunday – well, let us just say it was not one of mother's good days.
For that optic nerve of ecumenicity, the love of Christ for his Church,
for the image of Pope John XXIII, we had to wait until, appropriately
enough in the city of William Booth, it came from the gallant little
contingent from the Salvation Army. Patiently, and a little bewildered,
they had sat through our debates (the Mods and Rockers, Ecumaniacs
and Ecumoaners, with their razor-edged arguments and bicycle-chain
amendments) – as we clobbered one another with Calvin's *Institutes* or
the Thirty Nine Articles, and argued whether the one 'I'm alright Jack'
of Church History was named Calvin or Wesley. But with simple
prayer 'in the Spirit' and moving personal testimony, they showed us

evangelical religion at its best: evangelical, but catholic too. They were our Franciscans.
('"Splendidly Bonkers" at Nottingham', in *Methodist Recorder*, 1 October 1964)

* * *

At the Sheffield Conference, during the discussion of the proposals for a united British and American Methodist Church, I ventured the remark, 'Blest be the ties that bind, woe to the ties that choke!' I have often been warned by the sobersides that Methodism doesn't like people to try to be funny, but some of us keep feebly trying because, goodness knows, humour is not in superabundant supply, and the number of wits among us is small compared with those of us who have received half-portions.[15]
(*Methodist Recorder*, 19 November 1964)

1965

Historical and eschatalogical, temporal and eternal, these belong together. Snap the tension, and one of two disasters follows. Either the New Israel 'after the flesh' is equated with the New Israel 'after the spirit', and the visible, institutional Church is equated with the City of God – opening the way to clericalism and secularization, of which church history offers sad, ugly and plain examples. Or else, the unity of the one People of God dissolves into isolated pockets of purely spiritual religion, a view of the Church which in the end is docetic and sectarian. Thus nineteenth-century Protestants were wont to pick their ancestors a little choosily among the 'Reformers before the Reformation', Waldensians, Franciscans, Wycliffites and the like.

There is some truth at the heart of this. History often supports the great platitudes, the common myths rather than the paradoxes of historians, always prone to think, as Coleridge said, that they have

---

[15] Perhaps an unconscious echo of Sir Thomas More in his letter to Peter Gillies prefaced to *Utopia*: 'Some are so grimly serious that they disapprove of all humour, others so half-witted that they can't stand wit.'
(Penguin Classics, translation by Paul Turner, p.31)

struck a light when they have only snuffed a candle. It *is* among rebel minds and minority groups that we find emerging values.
(Introductory essay in *A History of the Methodist Church in Great Britain*, Vol.1, p.xiii)

Even in the hours when darkness and sin have abounded, when the divine society seems to have capitulated to the pressures of the world, the fundamental work of the Church has gone on, and, despite unworthy ministers and faithless people innumerable souls have been made partakers of the means of grace and of the hope of glory. It does no extra honour to the John Wesleys of the Church to forget the Parson Woodfordes and the Sydney Smiths, and to omit to say of them too, and of their labours – 'What hath God wrought?'! For in the Church's history it is the great, over-all picture that counts, and not this or that man, or movement or denomination or communion, nor indeed a cross section of the whole Church militant here on earth at any one point in time, but the whole purpose of God, to whom alone belongs the true glory.
(Ibid, p.xvii)

It is the daunting task of the historian not simply to look back, but, as far as may be, to put himself in the stream of events and to look forward to catch the full shock of the unpredictable. Just as the preceding works of J. S. Bach do not really prepare us for the *Matthew Passion*, though when we possess the masterpiece it has a quality of inevitability, and in the light of it we study his earlier work with deepened understanding – so it may be with history. A far-seeing man in 1700 might have pointed to this or that symptom of renewal – he could not have anticipated John Wesley.
(Ibid, p.xviii)

That John Wesley was able to look upon the whole world as his parish owed more than he knew, or most Methodists have ever acknowledged, to the devotion of [his father] who for more than forty years looked upon his parish as the whole world . . . Above all, in his concern for discipline ('what we have left of it') is he the heir of the Puritans and the father of the early (but scarcely of the modern) Methodists.
(Ibid, pp.xxiii, xxiv)

If the story of the Evangelical Revival without Samuel Walker and William Grimshaw would be *Hamlet* without Rosencrantz and Guildenstern, without John and Charles Wesley it would be *Hamlet*

without the Prince of Denmark and Horatio (to say nothing of Samuel Wesley as Hamlet's father's ghost!).
(Ibid, pp.xxvii-xxviii)

Herrnhut was, for all its startling missionary fervour, a kind of Protestant monasticism. Neither at City Road London, nor in the New Room, Bristol, or at Newcastle, did Wesley attempt anything similar. He was much more the Protestant friar – for what in the Moravian settlement was rooted in one place Wesley flung across the nation in a living connexion. Wesley's borrowings were never indiscriminate and we may be thankful that he did not import the Teutonic addiction to trombones, that he eschewed as unprofitable to pious English ears the sounding brass and tinkling cymbals of Moravian festivity, while imitating their charity.
(Ibid, p.xxxv)

* * *

Both unbelief and Christian apologetic are recondite and feeble compared with that of my undergraduate days in King's College, London, when you could hear Hilaire Belloc against H. G. Wells, G. K. Chesterton debating with Bernard Shaw, and Bishop Gore with Bertrand Russell. There is at this point a vulnerability, an uneasiness in Christian consciences, the awareness of how often and how disastrously in the past the Christians have fought losing rearguard actions in what they believed to be the defence of the faith but which to the outsiders looked like their own vested interests. In these ecumenical days we emphasize that the true task of the Church is to bear the form of a servant in the wider community.
('Christian Learning – the Great Tradition', in *Christianity in Education*, p.66)

Christians have things to say about education and society which do not depend on how few or many Christians are within it. Perhaps one of our great needs in theology is a new statement of natural law.
(Ibid, p.68)

[Late medieval scholasticism] Today nobody would understand the scholastic achievement: those 'cathedrals of the mind' – the decorated Gothic of St Thomas, the splendid fan tracery of Scotus, the austere perpendicular of Occam. Yet it became a closed world, not pushing back the frontiers of knowledge, but exploring by dialectical methods the implications of truth already given.
(Ibid, p.73)

Despite the immense gesture towards intellectual freedom of John Milton's *Areopagitica*, for most seventeenth century Christians truth was still a fugitive and cloistered virtue, and the new scientific virtues of curiosity, scepticism and freedom seemed to them much more like the qualities of original sin.
(Ibid, p.76)

It is well known that for the most part professors are rather simple middle-aged and elderly gentlemen who have got over enough successes and disappointments to give reasonably disinterested judgments, which cannot always be said of young university politicians, full of frustrations, who have prematurely abandoned learning for administration.
('Christian Learning – the University Revolution', in ibid, p.98)

This failure to distinguish between research and learning is one of the more obvious defects of the Robbins Report. We all know how futile and narrow some research can be, the pursuit of the unreadable by the unteachable, those eager beavers crying Ha! Ha! among the footnotes. Yet we should welcome the emphasis in the Robbins Report and elsewhere on the importance of post-graduate studies and the extension of what we might call the slightly higher degrees.
(Ibid, p.99)

1966

The exciting thing about human beings, and a reason for the historical study of great men, is to seek the 'x' in their equation, the point at which they cease to be explained by heredity and environment and the thought-world of their contemporaries.
('Luther: the Contemporary Image' in *Just Men* (1977) p.33)

'Mysticism' is perhaps the most nebulous word in the whole Christian vocabulary. It is a word which has fallen among thieves in its long journey from the Jerusalem of Christian sanctity to the Jericho of modern pantheist religiosity. Others will play the Good Samaritan in our Congress; it is rather for me, if not, like the Priest, to pass by on the other side, at least, like the Levite, to take one shuddering glance and hurry on.
(Ibid, pp.37-8)

[Luther] gives us a compass . . . he does not, as later Protestant orthodoxy, draw a map.[16] He is like some splendid painting by Turner of Venice in the clouds and sunshine: theirs is like a weather report from the Italian meteorological office.
(Ibid, p.41)

The great seminal studies of our time have not been in the main directed or commissioned dissertations, though I am all for keeping in touch across the world with what research is going on, and avoiding overlapping and wasted time. But for the rest let our motto be that of Nicodemus, 'Spiritus ubi vult spirat', rather than envying the Centurion, marshalling research students with 'Dico huic: vade, et vadit; et alii: veni, et venit.'
(Ibid, pp. 42-3)

I think we have to ask whether Luther (and not Luther alone, but most men of his age) did not pass on to his followers a view of pure doctrine and its relation to error which was not that of the mind of Christ, but which in fact appeared in the late second century, and from which the Churches in our time are struggling to be free.
(Ibid, p.44)

* * *

However much the Victorians rejoiced in the light, whether of reason or of faith, they were all to some degree conscious of the encircling gloom. We need always to remember the polarities of optimism and pessimism, of belief and unbelief and half-belief, the corrosion of older certainties in minds like Carlyle and Froude and Ruskin, the muted trumpets of 'In Memoriam'.
('Newman through Nonconformist Eyes', in *Just Men* (1977), p.138)

Newman was the Rembrandt of a Tractarian school at the heart of which was theological chiaroscuro. The darkness was Protestantism, the errors of the Reformers, and to compare Newman with John Adam

---

16 Cf *The Old Reformation and the New*, pp.18-19, where he adds: 'Or rather, his is not so much a map as an ocean chart – or like those curious maps of the Western Desert in World War II where there were few markings, but simply indications that "here the going is good . . . or bad . . . or fair". For the life of faith there is genuine pioneering, adventure. Nobody has ever lived where we live, at this point in time.'

81

Mohler is to feel that Anglo-Catholic polemic had, in this regard, obtusenesses and blind spots and rigidities beyond those of the Church of Rome.
(Ibid, p.145)

Nineteenth-century evangelicalism was further from Calvin than it knew, and its Calvin something infected by its passage from the age of William Perkins through the eighteenth-century Evangelical tradition – as any comparison between Karl Barth and modern Evangelicalism reveals . . . I myself would distinguish rather sharply between doctrines of the Reformers and what nineteenth-century Protestants conceived to be the Principles of the Reformation.
(Ibid, pp.148-9)

. . . Newman's defence of Private Judgement – not in his polemical essay on the subject, but in places in the *Apologia* where he asserts there is an awful never-dying duel in the Church between Authority and Private Judgement – 'alternately advancing and retreating as the ebb and flow of the tide': which, if it irresistibly recalls the Mock Turtle and the Gryphon in *Alice* – 'will you, won't you, will you, won't you' – defends perhaps all that Protestants ought ever to have defended, apart from the grave questions of religious liberty and the duty to obey one's conscience.
(Ibid, pp.149-50)

* * *

At the end Muntzer seems to have rejected the appeal to the big battalions. In his last poignant letter to the men of Muhlhausen, he bids them take the long view and look below the surface of events. And after four centuries this is what their successors in Eastern Germany are trying to do. A few months ago I stood in the Town Hall of Zwickau, where there is written on the wall in huge letters a facsimile of Muntzer's signature – 'Thomas Muntzer – qui pro veritate militat in hoc mundo.'[17] And as I listened to the Communist Oberburgomeister telling of his Christian upbringing, his disillusionment with bourgeois

---

[17] In *Patterns of Reformation* (1969) p.250, Rupp indentifies this quotation as the words of a receipt signed by Muntzer 'for his none too generous stipend' and comments: 'Perhaps he would have liked that to be the epitaph of one of the most fascinating and tragic of God's delinquent children.' Cf ibid, p.247 for a variation of the passage that follows.

Protestantism, his time in a concentration camp as a Communist, and as he threw at me sentences from the teaching of Jesus, I thought I heard the ghost of Thomas whispering: 'Endlich – at last, my peasants have won their war.' And though we should not accept the grievous over-simplification which divides East and West into godly and reprobate, the society of 'Gemein nutz' against that of 'Eigen-Nutz', this surely may be said. In Thomas Muntzer, as in no other Reformer, we touch that smothered undercurrent of pain and injustice which would one day explode in modern revolutionary man, one-sided, heretical, but something to which the Church, by reason of its own failure of compassion, cannot return an unqualified 'No'. Thomas Muntzer, like the Churches on the other side of the Iron Curtain, should give us an uneasy conscience.
('Thomas Muntzer: prophet of radical Christianity', *Bulletin of the John Rylands Library*, Vol.48, pp.486-7)

* * *

Now and then there are those who enter the John Rylands Library in mistake for Manchester Cathedral: an innocent error and, indeed, plausible, with the Gothic arches and the storied windows. And though it is not on record that anybody has addressed the Librarian as 'Mr Dean', that too would be a plausible ascription.
(*Bulletin of the John Rylands Library*, Vol. 49 No.1, Autumn 1966, p.2)

1967

Not the least important fact about Communism is that within it there has been an unresolved tension between a 'Rights of Man' idealism and the ideological system of Karl Marx.
(*The Old Reformation and the New*, p.2)

A good deal of what is called 'the New Reformation' – not least its rather naive self-confidence and its romanticizing of unbelief – would more appropriately be called 'the New Enlightenment'.
(Ibid, p.5)

If we rush back into history with our own questions and preoccupations we make the past a mere sounding-board for our own ideas, and substitute for the enthralling dialogue between generations a ventriloquial monologue through straw puppets of our own devising.
(Ibid, pp.5-6)

'Balanced judgment' at the lower end of the scale may stand for the dilettantism of the academic mind, for the evasion of prophetic action, for the man who flies to his packet of historical labels whenever there is a danger of meeting a new idea, rather like a very young medical student who might flee to his textbook and be more jubilant to have made his diagnosis and found the name of the disease than if he had made a cure. But rightly to discriminate between the present and the past, to press home an historical analogy does indeed demand a knowledge, a skill and a delicacy comparable with that of a surgeon operating on a brain. This is clear when we turn to the great historians. They really do call old worlds into being to redress the balance of the new. And even a working historian may have his use at a time like the present, of publicity explosions and of theological bandwaggons. He at least ought not to be shocked or surprised, or swept off his feet, and should be among the last to panic. And then, there is something in this business of historical perspective. The historian is made a freeman of the centuries, disengaged from the persistent fallacy of automatic progress, aware that Plato and Shakespeare and Beethoven and Wordsworth had perceptions of truth and beauty beyond most of us, and therefore for him there is a genuine continuing dialogue between the generations. There is much in the life of our own day which is peculiar to it – this was true of ancient Athens and medieval London. There are questions we must raise for ourselves and answer by ourselves, to which the voices of other generations are, to coin a phrase, irrelevant and immaterial. But there are other questions, and these the most profound, which touch all human experience, and to answer which involve us a continuing dialogue which we did not begin and which will go on after us, and then it may be that Augustine or Pascal or Dostoievski or Peguy may disconcertingly and freshly intervene.
(Ibid, pp.7-8)

[The Bible in the Reformation] . . . sometimes, as in the case of Luther's Bible, Tyndale's New Testament and the Czech Bible and the Authorized Version, a monument of beauty striking deep into the language and life of nations. But above all, speaking directly to men, through the power of the Holy Spirit, self-authenticating, a kind of 'Do-it-yourself' Christianity, working at all levels of society from the lovely vellum New Testament, which Queen Anne Boleyn loaned to the ladies of the court, to the copy which the boy Mekins hid under the stable straw until he could read it dangerously by candlelight, and in secret.

And not only the new Bibles printed in many hundreds of thousands, but with them illustrations – some of them not much above the quality of a strip cartoon, some of them splendid and beautiful – but

a reminder to our own age that it is no good having a 'Feed the Minds' campaign unless you have a 'Feed the Imagination' campaign alongside.
(Ibid, p.24)

In our time catechisms are at a discount, as well as learning by rote, but it is important to observe how much they counted, in the 16th century, as a method of communication. Catechetical teaching had, as the reformers knew, a respectable pedigree . . .
And at least the first Reformation catechisms were called by a modern enough word 'Dialogue'. They are, of course, frozen food, which is no substitute for fresh, even when warmed up. But if it is still permissible to suppose that there is a core of mathematics and language, which at some time must be remembered and learned by heart, then there is something to be said for learning a staple of theology and ethics when young, and disposing of this at a time when all learning is a bind!
(Ibid, pp.28-9)

We cannot jump from the 16th to the 20th century, or ignore the important elements in the 17th and 18th centuries which we might call an intervening crisis of integrity. Through its own failures of nerve and compassion, the Church lost its hold on two coherent human traditions, one in truth, in science, letters and philosophy, the other in social justice, traditions which by the end of the 18th century were in conscious opposition to the Church, one-sided, atheistic and anti-clerical.
(Ibid, p.50)

The Bishop of Woolwich sees a parallel between himself and Martin Luther, whose 95 Theses were also caught up in a publicity explosion. I wish him well. He has now only to be unfrocked, tried and condemned for high treason, to write four of the world's classics, to translate the Bible and compose a hymn book, and to write some 100 folio volumes which 400 years hence will concern scholars all over the world, and to become the spiritual father of some thousands of millions of Christians – to qualify as the Martin Luther of a New Reformation. One wishes that such weighty matters could be isolated from our modern publicity explosions. The kind of balloon-like inflation which television, Sunday newspapers, weekly journals and commentators give to whatever is sensational, controversial, and above all debunking to any kind of Establishment or orthodoxy, has been extended not only to the Beatles and James Bond, but to their theological and liturgical equivalent. This does not seem to me to be a healthy atmosphere. I prefer Rembrandt's

'Philosopher' as an image of how new truth appears. But it always sounds reactionary to criticize a new look, and I have a lively sense that to attack rebels is to sound like the Grand Inquisitor.
(Ibid, p.51)

As St John might have said: 'I write unto you, young men, because you know this present age, and because you are vulnerable; I write unto you, middle-aged, because you have learned another wisdom from hard knocks, because you are irritated at having to reopen questions that you solved for yourself years ago, and because, in your hearts, you too are unsettled by the thought that you may have missed the bus. I write unto you, supernumeraries, because you know how few are the ideas which really count, when you are packing them up for eternity.
(Ibid, p.53)

Of course we must streamline our church programme, find new energy and flexibility for activities outside church buildings. But let us not naively suppose that a Go-Go Christianity, all spontaneity and improvisation, will be necessarily effective either . . . The test of a living Church is how far it bears the form of a Servant, which is a hidden form known only by faith. The Church on earth is always Cinderella, dirty and ugly among the ashes, and her history an affair of pumpkins, field-mice, lizards – and only faith can see beneath the rags the Bride adorned for her husband. The Church too is a hospital where bad people are made good, and sinners forgiven. If it is thronged by the elderly, while the mature and young go off in motor-cars, it is perhaps because when men reach the 'Bay of Storms' in their sixties on the voyage of life, and meet serious illness either singly or with their wives, theirs is an existential need. The test is not whether services are exciting, up-to-date, experimental or impressively alert to recent intellectual discussion. A tiny group of rather dull people in some down-town chapel, coping with raising inordinate sums of money to keep going a building with damp and peeling walls, unappetizing and off-putting – may still reveal all the hidden majesty of God, be where grace is offered. I am all for experiments, for lovely new churches, for fine music, for exciting and moving liturgy. But I know that in the moment when a man's sins have found him out, or when he has to face the fact of cancer, all these things are completely irrelevant.
(Ibid, pp.61-2)

We have seen in Vatican II the brave sight of a great Church beating Protestant platitudes into Catholic epigrams, discovering freshly for

themselves things which, with Protestants, have become law and letter rather than Word and Spirit.
(Ibid, p.66)

They were men who made the Reformation, some of them great men and a few of them giants. I see Luther as Michelangelo's giant figure of Jeremiah – the great introvert; and Calvin as his Ezekiel, his arm gesturing towards the world; and Zwingli, assuredly Isaiah; and Bucer as Jonah, the missionary; and even Thomas Muntzer as a Daniel come to judgment. Today we need all the prophetic voices of the past.
(Ibid, p.67)

1968

In Sixteenth Century Europe where hunger and plague were daily in the streets, a terrifying amount of Christian energy went into angry theological polemic, and into rows of learned tomes, endlessly repetitive in argument. But at least this was not tithing dill, anise and cummin, about chalices or little glasses, about 'When is fermented wine non-fermented wine?', but a concern to guard the heart of the Christian gospel, both in worship and in preaching, what it means to set forth Christ 'as evidently crucified before men's eyes'.
(Book review, in *Methodist Recorder*, April 25, 1968)

* * *

This was Gordon Rupp's Presidential year and the following extracts are from his address to the Methodist Conference:

Granted that a remote and ineffectual don has any right to speak to you – which I admit is a question – at least as one whom our Church has set aside to rub his nose in Church History for many years, I may begin as a working historian. If I begin by being obscure and dull, some of you must be patient. We shall get to the four-letter words before the end.

Of course the Church must live and act 'now'. This is our moment on the stage and we must speak our own part. There is no substitute for learning the language of the present . . . Only, of course, it isn't quite 'now' . . . The arrow is flown, the moment is gone, as we sing. People today walk round with dead men's eyes and dead men's hearts. Remember that we all go about with dead men's words and could not frame an intelligible sentence without them, and in touching their words we cannot escape making contact with their ideas. If we suppose that we can make up our minds as we go along, plucking ideas out of the air, we do grievously err.

In art and letters there is a well-known way in which a generation leap-frogs over the last and lands on the last but one. A result of this is a kind of Carnaby Street theology, brightly coloured and up-to-date, but which on close examination turns out to be second-hand and a little grubby.

For the Christians to turn their back on history would indeed be to re-mythologise the gospel. I am not competent to begin to criticize New Testament scholars of our time on their own ground. But I prick up my ears when they say, as they seem more and more inclined to do, 'The historian does this . . . The historian does that,' or 'This is the historical method.' For, in fact, often this is not how historians behave at all, and good historians would not be half so sceptical as they are about finding the facts of the past, and much more sceptical than they are of their own capacity to pronounce on hidden motives of the heart. I would hesitate to make the kind of generalization about the mind of Henry VIII or Martin Luther which they do about the mind or even the mistakes of Our Lord.

However necessary the reaction against inward-turning pietism, the Church is more than a launching pad from which to take a running jump into the modern world.

So long as the Lord of the Church still says 'Include me in,' I have also to say I am

Gathered into the fold
With thy people enrolled
With thy people to live and to die.

There are times when Christianity becomes so entangled with things that the Spirit seems to say, 'Rub it out and do it all over again.' That is what he said to St Francis of Assisi . . . St Francis went naked to follow the naked Christ, and for love of him. At least one of the first band of his followers died of starvation. But this was gospel, not law. But a hundred years later came the Spiritual Franciscans, as they were called, and what moved them was not in the end love of Christ, but that they had a thing about poverty and went round railing at their fellow Christians and demanding that other people should sell all they had and give to the poor. And this was not gospel, but law. But in the end it is the gospel, not the law, which opens men's hearts and purses to give cheerfully, pressed down and running over.

I have spent a good deal of time in recent years studying the radicals of the Reformation period, many of whom for four hundred years had almost been forgotten. And why forgotten? Not, I think, just because they were persecuted by those who were scared by new ideas. But perhaps also because too much of their programme was negative rebellion against the Establishment. They were very good about dishing

88

out virulent abuse – I think the modern term is 'abrasive compassion' – but thin-skinned when it came to taking it, and almost naively unselfcritical. They ascribed freely the worst motives to those whom they attacked, though their own were not always above suspicion, for as Charles Smyth says, 'there are times when a young man on the make can do very well in opposition.' They were not so much the salt of the earth as its mustard. In the end their Christianity was under the Law.

One hundred and thirty years ago, two great institutions were opening new buildings at the rate of nearly one a month. One was the Methodist Church; the other British Railways. And for the same reason: they had to go where the people were, and where they were moving. And because, in that drab age, as it says in *Alice*, multiplication and uglification went hand in hand, the industrial parts of England became covered with railway stations which looked rather like churches and churches which looked rather like railway stations, and Central Halls like stone pork pies but more glorious within . . . But now both institutions face the question which G. K. Chesterton put in his telegram to his wife: 'I am here. Where ought I to be?' We can see where we ought to go: to the new housing estates, though what we should do when we get there is another question . . .[18]

Since your President is one . . . who has been fed week by week by the comradeship of good and unpretentious Methodist people, I draw attention to Soren Kierkegaard's picture of the Knight of Infinite Resignation, the Knight of Faith, and how close he comes to the average suburban Methodist type – so ordinary and so solidly earthed, that only when you look closely can you see, like the slight tremble of a ballet dancer when she alights, that here is life in another dimension, hid with Christ in God.

Let us not underestimate the wealth of goodness, quality of mind and practical know-how which still exists in the midst of the structured Church, or exaggerate the extent to which it has been a kind of hermit crab. And may I say to preachers among you: Most men at some time need the Law preached to them. All men at all times need the gospel.

[*On the Anglican-Methodist Conversations:*] There are those who profess to find it all boring . . . But who are we that we should not even be bored, when greater men than we, like William Temple and George Bell, shortened their lives by pouring energies into such a cause? In God's household we all have to take our share in peeling the potatoes.

18 Cf *Last Things First* (1964) pp.46-7

Some of us may need to hold our tongues – and to them I recommend a medicine of my own, the daily recitation of Psalm 39, the committee member's psalm.

We have in our ministry young men of quality, who would be the glory of the Church in any age, and we look to them to do for the coming age what perhaps my generation ought to have done and may have failed to do. But at the moment, God forgive us, they seem like a swimming bath where all the noise, the shouting and the splashing is coming from the shallow end.[19] We look to them for Valiants for Truth and Greathearts. We have enough Mr Talkatives and Mr Zeal of the Land busy

In the past thirty years English Christians have been able to look on while in other lands the Church had to face the gravest and most subtle of all temptations, that of identifying itself completely with an ideology, or a national way of life, or with one class or one race. We have watched a gallant minority resist the temptation and pay the price. We have witnessed widespread Christian failure: in Nazi Germany; beyond the Iron Curtain; in the deep South of North America, in South Africa and in Rhodesia. Now we have this same temptation laid upon the whole conscience of our whole Church.
(*Methodist Recorder*, June 20, 1968)

* * *

No doubt the differences between our world and that of St Benedict are more obvious than the similarities. But when David Knowles tells us that it was a 'new, adolescent, uncultivated age, of shifting landmarks and peoples', it rings a bell. For there is nothing more ironical than our way of speaking of mankind coming of age, and of mature Christianity – of a moral and spiritual progress contradicted by almost all the facts, when in fact ours is an age of adolescence, where, in things of mind and spirit, leadership has passed to the two great

---

19   In response to an open letter from Dr John J Vincent, Rupp wrote in the *Recorder* of July 25th: 'I will not withdraw "shallow end", but I do not think in terms of groups and huddles as you appear to do. I know that some young men who were not very good students and have not been very good circuit ministers, seem to have found in this radical programme a band waggon. I find many more of their contemporaries, who never get into print, who have more brains and more guts and to date have sacrificed at least as much. It requires no great hyper-sensitiveness to give away money belonging to other generations. When some of you really go Franciscan, as distinct from the muddled Christian socialism, some of us will sit up and even be moved to imitate you.'

overgrown schoolboy nations, America and Soviet Russia. For adolescence, as the late Professor Victor Murray once wrote, does not mean so much what happens to the young people between 14 and 22 as their sense of being surrounded with problems with which, out of their own inner intellectual and emotional resources, they are unable to cope, a world of instabilities and moods and uncertainties. By calling 'adolescence' the mark of our society I do not intend disparagement to the youth of today. I find more of the spirit of St Benedict in the young who sit down on the pavements in Downing Street and Whitehall and Westminster than in those who sit behind desks inside.
('St Benedict, Patron of Europe', a lecture delivered in Coventry Cathedral, in *The Church Quarterly*, July 1968, p.13)

To build an Ark, not made with hands, into which, two by two, human and eternal values might enter, to be kept until the waters assuaged and then brought safely out into a new world, this was the achievement of St Benedict, and that Ark was his Rule.
(Ibid, p.14)

It is the primary call to the Christian that he deny himself and take up his cross, that he must lose his life if he would save it, and that at all costs he must seek first the Kingdom of God. Forget these priorities, and the Church is submerged in an involvement which is always a two-way traffic; it becomes adjectival to a way of life, Gothic or American or British or European . . .   And false involvement begets false disengagement, the introverted pietism of Catholic asceticism or Protestant Puritanism.
(Ibid, p.15)

In contrast to the current 'kitchen sink' school of prayer of which we have so much on the radio at ten to eight, the spate of pseudo-Quoist which bids fair to become as depressing in this decade as pseudo-T. S. Eliot was in the last, St Benedict insists firmly that there shall be a place where nothing is put and nothing done but Prayer.
(Ibid, pp.15-16)

At least the Psalms remind us that their language, which has been at the heart of the main Christian tradition, has more about it of poetry than prose, more of the imbalance and extravagance of a love letter than of the formal precision of a notice board.
(Ibid, p.17)

* * *

From the President's New Year 'mini-encyclical':
We seem to be trying to turn our ministers into professional laymen, and our laymen into amateur ministers.

At a time when astronauts are launching out into the deep, we remember the importance of experimental ministries, by ministers, laymen, groups as well as individuals, who would erect Christian space stations between the Church and our secular society. But it would be disastrous if the astronauts become cut off from the great company at the launching site which made their venture possible, which sustain it with their skill, and which rejoice most of all at their success. It would be disastrous for the Church if our astronauts thought of themselves, or if we thought of them, as individuals doing tip-and-run raids into eternity rather than as the whole Church of God focussed at this point in time.

In spite of all the Christian hypochondriacs among us, hugging their dismal medicine bottles and their often indecipherable prescriptions, I believe our Church is 'Yet Alive!'
(*Methodist Recorder*, December 26, 1968)

1969

As the Anglican-Methodist negotiations neared their climax, the President put three questions to those who, like the 'Voice of Methodism', had serious misgivings about union with the Church of England:

After twelve years' discussion is there any other possible way which has been explained which could satisfy the consciences of Methodists and of Catholic and Evangelical members of the Church of England? How long, then, shall we go on talking, and is not the time for decision and action at hand?

All of us have difficulties, doubts, and there are obvious grave and complicated problems, but are not these problems and difficulties of a kind which can be better resolved together during Stage One and in the entirely new atmosphere which will be engendered by the commitment of two great Churches, one to the other?

Those of us who are older and ought to realise that we are not likely to see Stage Two ourselves, should surely take into consideration the young men in the ministry and the young people in our Church. May we not now be doing something which will enable them to fulfil their calling in a better Church more fitted to serve the coming age?

The Church of England moves in a mysterious way her wonders to perform, and perhaps it is not strange that our machinery, which is only about 150 years old, should be simpler than one which goes back to Anglo-Saxon times.
(*Methodist Recorder*, February 27, 1969)

* * *

His address to the Ministerial Session of the 1969 Methodist Conference was on the Pastoral Office:
If you read Psalm 78, that long rigmarole which goes on and on, rather like the 'Nightmare song' in *Iolanthe*, and which indeed from the realism with which it views the tragic history of Israel might well be called 'the Nightmare Song of the People of God', you will find there is a golden thread running through it all. Despite the rebellion, the ingratitude, the disobedience, the treachery of God's people, the end product is David, the shepherd king . . .

There is also Isaiah's shepherd Messiah, and the thirty-fourth chapter of Ezekiel: Ezekiel who is the J. S. Bach among the prophets and who in this great sonorous fugal passage interweaves judgment and mercy, splendidly and sombrely, in the minor key, save for the last great major chord – 'And you, my sheep, the sheep of my pasture, are men and I am your God.' And then there is the twenty-third Psalm – to the Church like the pavement in some ancient cathedral or the ambulatory in some venerable abbey, worn with the feet and knees of pilgrims: 'You are here to kneel where prayer has been valid.'
('The Pastoral Office in the Methodist Tradition', in *The Church Quarterly*, October 1969, p.119)

There is a painting by Peter Breughel which shows a shepherd with the sheep. He has everything a shepherd ought to have: wallet, rod, staff, hat. But he has his back to the sheep, who are being torn by wolves and scattered. The name of the picture is 'The Hireling'. He lacks the one essential of ministry: he does not care for the sheep. If the heart of our religion is love, reconciliation, compassion, caring to the point of sacrifice, then this is the bond between Christ's ministry and ours.

Without it all our training and our equipment, old or new, become gadgets and gimmicks. For if you have not charity, but only earnestness and zeal, then you become like the White Knight in *Alice*,[20] staggering

---

[20] Cf. p.106 for a different application of this simile.

from one lopsidedness to another, falling off your horse, either to the left or to the right, an ingenious inventor of new methods to meet hypothetical but untried situations, doomed to fail because situations mean nothing if you are not much more interested in the people involved in them.
(Ibid, p.120)

I am sure we must welcome all the help we can get from the sociologists, however much we deplore their addiction to the invention of foul language. I am sure, too, they need always to be checked by the historian, lest they take to vain prophesying, at which point sociology would cease to be a science and would degenerate into mythology undergirded by statistics.
(Ibid, p.121)

We have not to play down, but to emphasize, the ministry of the laity. The objection to a minister's becoming a bus conductor is not that it demeans the ministry, but that it may disparage the vocation of a bus driver. My Cornish society steward who drives a bus is the true worker priest, in his professional skill as a driver and mechanic, in the integrity with which he offers this to God, and in his relations with the people he meets day by day, which is truly, though he would never think like this, part of his pastoral office . . .

It has been a strength of our ministry that until very recently most of us came into it out of jobs, and we have had very few of those cloistered innocents – if that is the right expression – who have gone direct from school to university and then into a theological college. But let us not draw the conclusion from all this that a part-time ministry is preferable to or could supersede the need for a full-time one. There is no theological reason against part-time dentists, or part-time surgeons, but I would not trust my wife to one.
(Ibid, pp.123-4)

[*On the proposal for a Methodist episcopacy:*] I believe we should seize this opportunity to restore the centre of gravity to our Church, where it should always have been but where perhaps it no longer is, at the point of pastoral care, of shepherding the flock. It would, it seems to me, be fatal to begin with any ex-officio bishops, certainly not ex-presidents, or connexional officials, or college tutors. I don't believe our corridors of power and ambition are very large or very sinister, but at least let us rid ourselves of even the faintest reproach that these have

94

had any entrance at all in our midst. (Remember Lichfield![21])

We might perhaps have room after a bit for a scholar or an administrator or two, but not at the beginning. Nor would I for the most part choose Chairmen of Districts – though as far as in them lies they are fulfilling a true pastoral bishop's office. But . . . I should look for bishops at the place where historically our pastoral care has centred, to Superintendent ministers, the kind who get on with their colleagues, really look after their young men, and are respected and loved by their people . . . I imagine the situation would be like that in the early Celtic Church, when the administration was monastic, in the hands of abbots, and bishops were just kept to ordain – for breeding purposes, so to speak.
(Ibid, p.127)

* * *

There can never be a purely biblical theology: Luther's reference to the Apostles' Creed as his 'little Bible', and the debt of the Reformers to the theology of creeds and councils generally, show that the Bible needs for its interpretation the dogma it has helped to create. Despite an early violent reaction against philosophy the Reformers soon learned that men reject its help at the peril of being at the mercy of the unconscious habits of mind and presuppositions of their own age, for it is perhaps the de-mythologizing, not so much of the past as of one's own age, which is the real problem for the biblical theologian.
(*Patterns of Reformation*, p.xix)

Why this work [Erasmus's Greek New Testament] which had been planned and prepared for several years had to be so rushed at the last is another question, the more pointed since so many other works of Erasmus were finished at this headlong pace. No doubt the new rhythm of the printing age has something to do with it, or perhaps the well-known failure of nerve which besets scholars, leading them to jeopardize the patient research of years in a last frantic attempt to 'get the thing out'.
(Ibid, p. 10)

---

[21] A reference to the meeting in Lichfield in 1794 at which leading figures in the Connexion devised a plan for the appointment of Methodist bishops and proposed themselves as candidates for the office.

The manifesto [a petition to the magistrates at Basle in 1528] seems to have been supported by all the guilds save the Bread-bakers, the Smiths, and the Sailors and Fishermen (a nice problem for the Marxist historian!).[22]
(Ibid, p.36)

By refusing to apply univocally what the Old Testament said about images and idolatry to Christian use of pictures and statues, Luther's Protestantism, as distinct from Karlstadt's (and Zwingli's) Puritanism, left room for a whole dimension of beauty to be used in the service of God. Had his view prevailed, later Protestantism, not least in the 19th century, would have been spared the cult of what the Gryphon called Uglification and the 20th century rash abandonment of Puritanism for a secularized religiosity immersed in sentimental and second-rate vulgarity. It was, moreover, for Luther an essential point, which he would drive home in the spring of 1522, that a reform of these things by law alone or by outward violence could achieve nothing. The image must first be removed from the hearts of men – and then the superstition would disappear, and the objects of abuse would fall into disuse.
(Ibid, p.104)

We might feel that at this time Karlstadt was a very model of a modern intellectual, since these large gestures of solidarity with the workers were accompanied by a determination to hold on to his academic and ecclesiastical stipend . . . He startled his students by addressing them as 'dear colleagues' – for though the priesthood of all believers was by now a familiar theme, the vice-chancellorship of all undergraduates lay within the mists of four centuries ahead.
(Ibid, pp.112,113)

For Karlstadt, as for so much later Sabbatarianism, Sunday is a 'day of Rest – and sadness'. Even the inward, spiritual meaning of it with all the emphasis on the divine will and sanctifying energies, and the passiveness of the human heart, is preoccupied with states of the soul, and set throughout in the doleful, minor key. In the end Karlstadt's Sabbath is under the sign of the Law rather than of the Gospel.
(Ibid, p.130)

22 This point is elaborated in *Protestant Christianity* (1960) p.12.

Protestants, who perhaps pray 'for' their good causes more timidly, or at any rate less exuberantly, than their 16th century fathers, may find it difficult to understand how important for Luther was the notion of praying 'against' anything. For Luther this was a grim, final expedient, like the cane in a boys' school of other days.
(Ibid, p.132)

In the church of St Catherine, Zwickau, there survives today one small fragment of its medieval glass, a figure of St Stephen, that angry young man of the Primitive Church, whose fiery diatribe against the elders of Zion provoked his violent death. That is perhaps how Thomas Muntzer, sometime preacher in that church, would have seen himself, though it is hardly the image which has prevailed in Protestant history. There he has been, for most of the time, Luther's 'arch-devil of Allstedt' . . .
(Ibid, p.157)

Muntzer raises the question which later Protestants, from the days of the Huguenots to those of Dietrich Bonhoffer, were to press, having rejected Luther's passive doctrine: whether, in fact, there may not have to be drastic Christian action against tyranny, not least against a tyranny bolstered up by the religious guarantees of an obtuse Establishment.
(Ibid, p.248)

There is a long book-list in [Muntzer's] papers which includes most of the important tracts published 1518-19, and though it would be precarious to judge the mind of a modern parson from a Blackwell's catalogue found among his posthumous effects, and though the possession of all these writings would demand a high proportion even of a bachelor income, it is very possible that he did indeed own, or read, most of them.
(Ibid, p.252)

Achatius Glov, a Leipzig bookseller . . . seems to have been a kindly bookman, of that sort who so orders his shop that those who stand may read. He was aware of the tension in a young scholar's mind between the books he wants and those he can afford.
(Ibid, p.253)

The relation between Muntzer and Karlstadt is not unlike that between Brer Rabbit and Brer Terrapin in *Uncle Remus* (which Muntzer, who quotes Aesop's Fables, would, like Luther, have loved) –

Karlstadt's piety being like that of Brer Terrapin's existence which he described as 'lounjun' roin' en suffer'n'.
(Ibid, p.257)

The Peasants' War would have happened had there been no Thomas Muntzer, and it can be argued that, even in Thuringia, he had little influence on the course of events. Had he not been there, they would still have rebelled under other leaders and still have come inevitably to military disaster. None the less, the Peasants' War was, as we say, 'right up Muntzer's street'. It fitted admirably within his ideology. He had been prepared to work with the authorities. They had repudiated him. From now on, his levelling tendencies get the upper hand.
(Ibid, p.301)

[Muntzer] is the first great rebel against the new gospel – and this provokes him into the kind of one-sidedness of a John Henry Newman in reaction against a similar too-comfortable Evangelicalism in the 19th century . . . The similarities between Muntzer and Kierkegaard, often remarkable, are because the latter too was in reaction against a Lutheran Establishment. Muntzer's fierce dissatisfaction with the formal, over-clericalized religion of his day, the abuses of which were shared, he felt, by the new and reformed piety of Luther and his friends, led him to look for salvation beyond the bounds of what was generally regarded as Christendom; and his prophetic premonition of a new age, when the Word of God would come home to men from strange lands and strange people, has curious affinities with radical theology in our own time. Those who have thought of his violent activism as more like Mohammedanism, or the feudal, fighting Christianity of the age of the Crusades, are maybe as percipient as those who at the other extreme would dress him up in the garb of 20th-century revolution. At least his theology was born, like his faith, from his life in a revolutionary setting. Not reading or speculating, but living, dying and being damned, made him a theologian.
(Ibid, pp.303-4)

Cranmer restored to divine service the regular recitation of the whole Psalter, which ticks away like the second-hand, while the whole Bible is read more slowly, like the hour-hand of a clock.
(Ibid, p.306)

The national Reformation in England, and the tendency to liturgical uniformity in the Church of Rome after the Council of Trent, have obliterated the memory of the immense variety, bordering on anarchy,

98

of the liturgies of the Middle Ages. It was one of the merits of the German Reformation that it retained something of this diversity and flexibility.
(Ibid, p. 307)

* * *

It would not be fair to Luther to look at him only through the eyes of Erasmus. But it is true of all the great historical controversies – Newman and Kingsley is another case in point – that we do no service to one side by playing down the merits of the other, for this is a sure way to miss the human poignancy, and even the theological nerve of the encounter. We do not illuminate, we obscure the truth when we underrate the religion and faith of Erasmus.
(*Luther and Erasmus: Free Will and Salvation*, p.1)

Satirists are notoriously thin-skinned. They lie awake o' nights, brooding on lesser insults than they have dealt to their opponents.
(Ibid, p.2)

* * *

Sometimes a new Professor will use such an occasion as this to look before and after at the provision made for his subject in the University, and its future needs. But I have rather recently returned to Cambridge with something of the dazed rapture of a Jacob who, having settled down happily, and as he thought permanently, with Leah, finds himself suddenly transferred to Rachel's bosom, as yet too stunned to have got round to counting sheep in Laban's household. Then, too, my predecessors were called into the vineyard at the sixth and at the ninth hour, with time enough to criticize the management, but I at the eleventh had better simply study to be a labourer worthy of his hire.
(*Hort and the Cambridge Tradition*, an Inaugural Lecture delivered on 14 November 1969, pp.1-2)

Like all holders of the Dixie Chair, [Norman Sykes] knew that this English language of ours is first and foremost a musical instrument – and never a blunt tool, not a cosh, not a bulldozer.
(Ibid, p.4)

We may suppose that the indispensable quality of a historian is an imaginative scepticism, controlled by evidence.
(Ibid, p.10)

99

For the historian, '1066' is as important as the 'all that'. A recent writer discussing the theory of history mentioned that Luther appeared before the Diet of Worms in 1525, and since he repeated this wrong date four times on one page one could only suppose that, eminent historian though he was, he had either got this one wrong, or thought it too trivial to matter. Yet this cuts deep into the stuff of history: its irreversibility, the flow of time onwards and forwards. Germany in 1525 was vastly different from 1521 because of those earlier happenings, because of Luther, who he was and what he did. And also by reason of numbers of quite fortuitous happenings but for which we might now think of Martin of Wittenberg as another of those scholars like Henry Totting of Oyta or Perez of Valencia whom it is the latest one-upmanship to drag from well-deserved oblivion as the real clue-makers of the later Middle Ages.

History happens forwards, but it is recorded and remembered and interpreted backwards – and this is the tension of the historian's craft and its high moments, those salmon leaps of imaginative perception . . . Perhaps this is the high art of the historian, to sit down patiently before the evidence, to listen to it if it may be without preconceptions and forejudgment, until one hears undertones and undertones such as only a disciplined love of truth and, one might add, imaginative compassion can wring from the study of the past.

(Ibid, pp.11,13)

But if Hort was born free into a tradition of unfettered enquiry into which others could only be liberated at cost, it was not that there was no price to pay, but that it had been paid already. For behind the Cambridge Victorians, the classical scholars, the scientists, the poets, the divines, there stand those Cambridge Platonists whose image confronted Hort daily in the Chapel of Emmanuel with their reminder that the spirit of man is the candle of the Lord, and the light of truth unquenchable. And behind them, the Cambridge Puritans – like him of Christ's repudiating truth as a fugitive and cloistered virtue, or those others who like Hort himself were men of great learning well content to give a score of years and all they had of wisdom to the little people in small country parishes. And behind them too, the Cambridge Reformers who knew truth as that for which all men owe God a death.

(Ibid, pp.20-1)

If men may give their lives in pursuit of money, or ambition, or squander their gifts in endless trivialities, why should this man not spend his life in pursuit of truth? It would not go down well, I dare say, with the University Grants Committee if our University were altogether

100

composed of Horts. The credibility gap between Oxbridge and Plateglass and Moscow and Berkeley, California, is not likely to be bridged that way. But might it not in the long run be even more disastrous if we ceased to have room among us for such Men of Learning? And when we listen to a Robbins report with its painful confusion of learning and research, and its dreary vista of endless processions of eager beavers chasing an alphabetic jungle of slightly higher degrees, we want to say – 'Tell it not in Gath, rather tell the Department of Education and Science; whisper it not in the streets of Ashkelon – rather cry it aloud in the corridors of Westminster and Whitehall – that a University is a seat of Learning, and that in the long run wisdom is justified by her children.'
(Ibid, pp.21-2)

* * *

Two interesting receipts for Muntzer's stipend as a preacher in Our Lady's Church at Zwickau and at St Catherine's . . . are illuminating, for they show (as against the Marxist interpretation) that when he left Our Lady's church for the downtown weavers' church, it was for double the stipend!
('Muntzer's Writings', in *Journal of Ecclesiastical History*, Vol. 20, p.310)

1970

I once had a frightening experience in a church delegation in which I took a very minor part at the end of World War II, of penetrating to the very top level of the British Military Command in Germany. All the way up it was salutings and Sirs and Sergeant Majors and fences and rules and the rest of it; and then we found ourselves sitting on the edge of an office table where two Major Generals were talking on the telephone and it was 'Maurice' and 'Gerald' and 'Will you please pass this on to Monty?', talking by their Christian names. And I've noticed this ever since . . . When we get to the height of these complexities there is informality, there is friendship, there is a very simple kind of comradeship. As we look at the Twelve Disciples we realise that this too, of course, was true: it was true of Christ and his one Holy, Catholic and Apostolic Church . . .

This is the glorious liberty of the children of God. We mustn't miss this, or the things that Jesus was teaching as he tried to train the Twelve, as he told them the Sermon on the Mount (which really is not about

individuals, but about 'group dynamics' as we say, about the only way in which a community of people is either much worse or much better than the number of people who go to make it up). And you remember how hard it was for them to learn this lesson, how he had to take a little child and put him in the midst to show them. And when that didn't do he had to take a towel and wash their feet and that didn't show them. And in the end he had to take a cross, and then they began to understand.
('Sons of God', a sermon preached in the University Church, Cambridge, 22 February 1970)

* * *

I would not undervalue the generous ecumenicity of the Church of England. More than any Church she has taken costly and serious initiative with the Romans, Orthodox, Lutherans, Presbyterians, Free Churchmen. But at the end of the day, the grave question has to be asked whether the Church of England is capable of making up its mind, and then of doing it. For with all its faults, the Methodist Church is such a body. And so is the Church of Rome. Future historians, looking back on our times, may well conclude that the failure of the Church of England to respond to its own gesture, in 1968, marks the point where the spiritual initiative in England passed from the Church of England in the first place to the Roman Catholics and to the Methodists in the second.
('Chaos and Old Night', a comment on the tract *Growing into Union* by a group of Anglo-Catholics and Evangelical Anglicans; in *Frontier*, August 1970, p.175)

* * *

I do not defend the title 'The New Counter-Reformation' – lecturers are unjust stewards who sit down and write quickly in the hope of making friends with the mammon of unrighteousness by at least supplying a title, well in advance not only of lecturing, not only of writing, but even of thinking about it.
('The New Counter-Reformation', in *The Heythrop Journal*, 1970, p.5)

I find . . . in our contemporary scene only a lively and acid propaganda, conducted largely in paper-backs, newspapers and television, about which one is inclined to murmur: 'All publicity corrupts. Absolute publicity corrupts absolutely.'
(Ibid, pp.8-9)

One of the perils of our time may be the Catholic or Protestant 'ecumeniac' who leans over so far backwards to be eirenical that the historical rocking-chair is upset.
(Ibid, p.10)

How soon the barricades were up! The one sensible confrontation between Luther and Cajetan in October 1518 degenerated into a shouting match within minutes over a theological misunderstanding that in a better context a clear-headed undergraduate, if there is such a thing, could have resolved.
(Ibid, p.12)

One of the things we need is to face our Christian problems with balance and with judgment at a time when one-sided prophecy is more appealing to the ear. One of the features of the World Council of Churches at Uppsala last year, to my mind, was that the Church reflected a world swept by waves of giant irrationalisms, tensions of race and class, and youth versus age. In one way it was as though over Western and white Christendom the words 'Buy now, pay later' had come to judgment for the sins of past generations. It was fairly obvious that many of these problems were not capable of rational diagnosis or rational solution. At the recent meeting of the Central Committee of the World Council of Churches in Canterbury, it was the non-white Christian churches who pressed on the white ones a fierce resolution deploring the white failures and demanding reparation for the coloured peoples. I am sure this has to be listened to, and in penitence, by white Christians; but I am sure this is not good theology. Similarly with the claim made there that violence is justifiable in the search for justice, but with no attempt to elucidate (as the sixteenth century Jesuits laboured to find) a rationale of this, to set out the conditions and safeguards of such a doctrine. The ecumenical movement may need to turn away from its bureaucrats and to recall the theologians.
(Ibid, p.14)

1971

I know nothing about architecture: but when Sir Kenneth Clark stands beside a Wren building and murmurs the word 'Proportion' – and when I look at Trinity Library and the Gallery at Emmanuel, I get his point. And like architecture, true theology is a matter of proportion as in this [Athanasian] Creed statements balance one another, taking the stress one from the other in a manner very different from the lopsidedness of Christian 'god-talk' in the last 30 years . . .

The Emperor Charles V was one of the great rulers of empire, with vaster lands than any for five hundred years. But there came a moment when he realised that it was no good having a shopping list, for 1559 or 1971, when it is early closing day, and he decided to spend his remaining days fitting himself to meet his maker. And so to the great scene in Brussels Cathedral when the Imperial Herald read the long roll of his titles, and one by one he renounced them all, until he stood alone, a man humble before God.

('A God who speaks', a sermon preached in the University Church, Cambridge on Trinity Sunday, 1971)

1972

Ours is one of the most preached-at generations . . . When John Ruskin – that mixture of Robin Day and John Betjeman who would have revelled in BBC2 – was a small boy, he used to stand on a chair and preach to his parents. He had always the same text: 'People be good'. And so it is with our secular preaching which is always law rather than gospel. What past generations got from parsons we get from Bernard Levin and Malcolm Muggeridge, from tedious leading articles, especially in *The Guardian*, and from a whole series of television programmes which though they begin admirably: 'For amusement only', wind up by moralising upon social problems in a most boring way – from Dr Findlay through Dixon of Dock Green to Alf Garnett. (*The Word and the Words*, p.3)

In our time we have encouraged audience participation in worship, but when we all have to say the Blessing in unison and say together the Prayer of Humble Access we need to remember that it is not less truly corporate worship when in faith a silent congregation adheres to the voice of the minister; while the Black and White Minstrel technique of people bobbing up and down all over the place, generally inaudibly, is a device which rapidly palls.
(Ibid, p.6)

[God] keeps at every point the divine initiative. The other day I came across one of the more interesting student graffiti in Cambridge where a young man had scrawled on the wall what used to be called his declaration. 'I love you,' it read. And then I observed a few yards

further on, the devastating reply: 'Why?' – 'the wonder, why such love to me?'[23]
(Ibid, p.8)

We live in a time of transition and experiment, and I do not mean to sound carping when I say that many of them are rather like attempts to brighten cricket by widening the bat or altering the lbw rule or to clean up hooliganism by booking one or two players in football. I suppose that those who have discarded 'Thee' and 'Thy' for 'You' and 'Your' have the future on their side. When the Roman Catholics go direct to modern speech from the Latin I do not mind at all, and it is only when it is over-accentuated and self-conscious that it jars and irritates, as I confess it sometimes does. And for myself, I am too old to learn this new trick: having called God 'James' for sixty years, I am not going to change to 'Jimmy'. . . Very recently there have been prayers of a certain crisp chumminess as though the Lord and the preacher knew what the rather dumb members of their flock needed to be reminded of. There is, I feel, a difference between leaning on God and breathing down his neck, and I am not convinced of an improvement when we speak to God as a man speaketh to his milkman.
(Ibid, pp.13-14)

The literature of the Ecumenical Movement is, for me, a small cross. I fear its jargon, because it hides meaning. I hate its ecumenese, a lowest common denominator of broken English from all over the world with a teutonized German American predominating. Those memoranda and church reports soaked in the almost equally dirty language of sociology are a despair. And I am glad to turn with my grandchildren to Enid Blyton and Magic Roundabout.
(Ibid, p.14)

---

23 Using this illustration in his sermon on 'The Dimension of Depth' (*The Sixty Plus and other Sermons*, pp.79-80), he added: 'It was springtime, and as I came back that day another way, it was through the green pastures of the Backs, with flowers of green and yellow and purple and white. It seemed to me then that the whole splendour of spring is one of God's graffiti – his declaration to us all: "I love you" . . . And all the response of his children, all the music, all the prayers, all the liturgies, all the obedience, represent that wondering response, "Why?"'
Preaching in Great St Mary's, Cambridge on 22 February 1970, he adds another example of the graffiti he has seen along Pembroke Street: 'Hair needs comb, but not so much as comb needs hair', describing it as 'a very profound statement'.

1974

The rejection by the Church of England of re-union with the
Methodists in 1969 had its roots in the seventeenth century before
Methodism was, in the petrifying of the Catholic and Evangelical wings
of the Church of England, through the violence of 1640-60.
('Son to Samuel: John Wesley, Church of England Man', in *Just Men*
(1977) p.112)

Wesley regarded new words and slang as a compost heap: he did
not, as we do, consider them the garden. And he would have made
short shrift of our contemporary immersion in jargon, not least in the
ecumenical dialogue.
(Ibid, p.119)

Modern theologians may stagger from one lop-sidedness to another
– from transcendence to panentheism, from Scripture to existentialism –
for all the world like the White Knight in *Alice* whose progress was a
series of one-sided crashes (the theological name is, I think, 'polarity').
But Wesley knew how to lean over without losing his balance, and
when he tumbled, as once or twice he did, he landed on his feet.
(Ibid, p.122)

[Wesley] did not think of holiness as some nineteenth- and
twentieth-century movements have tended to do as a kind of vague
Scotch mist, but with the ordered colours of an English garden, the
flowers and fruits of the Spirit, each with a colour, and a shape and a
name.
(Ibid, p.127)

1975

Elizabeth did not care for Bishops: she could neither flirt with them
nor box their ears. They were perhaps rather a poor lot compared with
her great sea captains. They were of course a second eleven, and the
English Reformation story would have been very different had men
like Cranmer and Ridley and Rogers and Rowland Taylor not been
destroyed.
('Matthew Parker, a Man', in *Just Men* (1977) p.80)

* * *

Some day somebody will write an essay on 'Time and the Reformation', for the historical scene resembles a Dickensian image of a shop full of clocks all chiming and striking and whirring at different moments, going at different speeds. One needs to note the slowing up and acceleration of the Reformation and the different causes of it (e.g. the slowing down of Lutheranism in German cities after 1524 and the outbreak of the eucharistic controversy). It is always important to bear in mind in the case of England, the ten-year gap, the fact [that] in England 1527 is a key date compared with 1517 on the Continent. And by the 1540s this means that what happened in England and Scotland was affected by a whole spate of argument and happening, in the presence of a great literature of liturgical and theological change. ('The Europe of John Knox', in *John Knox: A Quartercentenary Reappraisal*, p.3)

Apocalyptic seems to recur in those moments in history when things come to the boil, and when a spiral view of historical development replaces the linear one of calmer days: in those periods when the sleeping volcano underlying human existence erupts, violence is in the air, and the irrational takes over. Such was Europe in the 1550s on the edge of a terrible period of religious war. (Ibid, p.4)

Knox marched towards the sound of the guns[24], Erasmus away from them. (Ibid, p.4)

Remembering Auschwitz and Berlin we may wonder . . . whether we have dismissed too easily the view that it is justice, measured in divine terms, whereby empires rise and fall, and without which, as Augustine saw, all power systems become 'robbers' caves' – the shattering truth that I belong to Glasgow, but Glasgow belongs to God. (Ibid, p.14)

* * *

In the autumn of 1945, Rupp had accompanied Bishop George Bell to Germany and was present at the meeting in Stuttgart with leaders of the German Evangelical Church. Their statement included the moving

---

[24] Cf p.6, where he adds the qualification, 'with butterflies in his stomach'.

declaration: 'We are the more thankful for this visit, because we know ourselves to be joined together with our people, not only in a solidarity (Gemeinschaft) of suffering, but also in a solidarity of guilt. With great pain do we say: through us endless suffering has been brought upon many peoples and lands . . .'

However one translated the difficult word 'Gemeinschaft' – as 'solidarity' or 'communion' – the sentence about solidarity of suffering and guilt rings out as a great 'For whom the Bell tolls' passage. Those who saw the Nuremberg criminals, led by Goering, come one by one to the microphone and say, 'Not guilty!' cannot but think of these others, most of whom had been in prison for the gospel, with their affirmation, 'Guilty!' Moreover, it has implicit in it a theology of reconciliation.

There are impasses in human relationships when the gesture of penitence must come from the offending side, a gesture which can never be demanded but which has to be a free initiative. Such was this gesture and this initiative, and it was accepted as having opened a new way, to the new solidarity of hope, within the fellowship of the ecumenical movement. It is a theology of self-accusation and of penitence, in the presence of God. One feels that there is still a good deal of thinking along these lines to be done in ecumenical circles, not least in regard to the whole theology of militancy which begins by accusing others, and which has room for penitence only in others.
(*'I Seek My Brethren': Bishop George Bell and the German Churches,* p.27)

In Berlin . . . there was a grim visit to the great railway station, the Lehrter Bahnof, with platforms and lines covered with thousands of human beings, mostly very old and very young, and teenage girls with bleeding, bandaged feet. I remember I found a bar of Dairy Milk chocolate and produced it, but Guy Clutton Brock, who was conducting us, said, 'Put that away or people will be killed fighting for it.' And I remember Bell going slightly ahead of us, not able to speak German to them, but stopping and smiling and patting children, and turning again and again to ask for facts and information – nothing to give but that obstinate compassion which persisted until the tiny streams of 'Christian Reconstruction' became the river we now know as 'Christian Aid'.
(Ibid, pp.27-8)

1976

In the military hospital of the Invalides, in Paris, the Emperor Napoleon Bonaparte lies in a majestic tomb of red porphyry upon green granite, surrounded by the Marshals of France and of the 'Grande Armee'. As Humpty Dumpty would say, 'There's glory for you!' But go from there to Assisi, to the little crypt where another 'Frenchie' – 'il francesco' – lies in his plain tomb in the grey travertine stone, surrounded by his companions, Brother Leo, Brother Masseo, Brother Angelo and Brother Rufino. No, *there* is glory for you! – the upsidedown glory of the Kingdom of God.
('St Francis of Assisi', in *Just Men* (1977), p.15)

Thirteenth century Christians had not the advantage of a public-school education: they knew less about a stiff upper lip than a trembling lower one. And though Dr Burkitt (Harrow and Trinity) produced a fine and sensitive translation of Francis's 'Canticle of the Sun', by no stretch of imagination could St Francis have written the Harrow school song 'Forty Years On'!
(Ibid, p.18)

When a mystic tells us what he saw, the rest of us have a right, almost a duty, to discuss questions of 'subjective' and 'objective'. But when a saint says that he sees – the rest of us had better keep silence and let our words be few.
(Ibid, p.26)

1977

If [Thomas More] had an Oxford wit, he had a Cockney sense of humour, not least in a certain dead-pan quality.
('Thomas More and William Tyndale', in *Just Men*, p.45)

I suppose most of us have a point of deep conviction, however humorous or compassionate we may be, when humour and compassion wither.
(Ibid, p.48)

Richard Ullmann, a modern German Quaker who survived the concentration camps, said to me about the outburst of satirical writing in Germany after 1945: 'Satire is the last refuge of those unwilling to face the Cross.'
(Ibid, p. 49)

The English language still bestrides the world – hanging over it like the grin on the face of the Cheshire Cat, after the British Empire has disappeared.
(Ibid, p.55)

* * *

As the rules of a sonnet make possible its spontaneity, and as the devotion of the ladies of Hefa is to be explained against a strict discipline, liturgical and ascetic, so the Puritan devotion of the heart was imbedded in an often complex rationalism, and is to be set against an austere pattern of religious life, in community, in family worship, in Bible study and in concern for conscience, as well as in adherence to the sacramental ordinances and the observance of the Sabbath . . .

In the last thirty years attention has centred on first one and then another aspect of Puritanism . . . Too little attention has been paid to their spirituality, to what they have to say of Christian experience, of their devotion to Christ, and about the joy of the Christian religion. But the evidence is abundant, at almost every level of religious and theological writing. It is time to look at Puritanism from the other side of the (Christopher) Hill.
('A Devotion of Rapture' in *Reformation, Conformity and Dissent,* p.119)

The appeal to violence, the Civil War and its aftermath, the events of 1660-2, have provided a distorting mirror to all of us who have come after, Anglicans and Free Churchmen. There was no doubt too a changing mood and temper of the age which was reflected in new kinds of Christian preaching. Certainly this religion of the heart seems to have disappeared, like an underground stream, to emerge in the Evangelical Revival. Perhaps it never wholly returned, and there are colours missing from the wide spectrum of English religion . . . The failure of much contemporary religion to meet not only the intellectual but also the emotional needs of men may have deep roots: a mere charismatic movement, loosely theologically orientated, would seem to have less prospect of meeting such needs than a christocentric piety with a properly Trinitarian theology.

When John Henry Newman reacted so sharply against the fervour of Frederick Faber and William Ward and stood a little aloof from their Italianate devotions, did this not represent something very Oxford and very English which had come to look upon rapturous devotion with suspicion?
(Ibid, pp.129-31)

* * *

In my lifetime we have not handled youth very well. What matters about Rupert Brooke is not what he wrote of Granchester, but what happened to his generation in Flanders and Gallipoli. Go and sit in the chapel of the Leys School and notice how the walls are ringed with the names of young men from 18 to 21 who died in a few months of leaving school and university. On Judgment Day when the nations are gathered together, what the 20th Century did with its young life must come terribly high on the agenda.
(From a sermon preached at the University Church, Cambridge, on the occasion of the Queen's Silver Jubilee, 5th June 1977)

1980

Donald English once gave a fine talk in which he spoke of God's 'difficult thoughts'. But he agreed when I said that what worried me were not God's hard sayings but his plain, simple ones, the ones that are so plain to see and easy to understand that we would most of us run a thousand miles away from them. And when we have acknowledged the problems about 'ministry in the New Testament', is there anything plainer than the wholeness of the life and ministry of our Lord, who took upon him the form of a servant, who came not to be ministered unto but to minister, who took a towel on his way to taking a Cross, who laid down his life for his friends, who was the Good Shepherd, who sanctified himself for the sakes of those yet to be brought into the fold?
('The "Wholeness" of our Ministry', in *The Epworth Review*, January 1980, pp.46-7)

* * *

'Mightier than an army is the power of an idea whose time has come' is a text on which a good many homilies about the sixteenth century might be written. But how ideas 'come' and 'go' in this sense – how, having been inert, commonplace and unimportant for long enough, they suddenly find their hour, and become living, moving forces in the minds, hearts and wills of masses of human beings – is a complex mystery. Much the same is true of the spread of ideas from time to time and from place to place. For ideas are like germs; they seem often to be carried by 'carrier patients' who are perhaps more dangerous than the fanatics or the prophets. And there certainly seem to be incubation periods at the end of which the authorities awaken to danger, finding themselves ill prepared with a plague on their hands . . . As every

111

Grand Inquisitor knows, it is easier to kill men than destroy their ideas. You never know when thoughts may be revived; and it has been well said that only God knows when a book is dead.
('The Battle of the Books: The Ferment of Ideas and the Beginning of the Reformation' in *Reformation Principle and Practice*, p.3)

The film producer Sam Goldwyn is said to have grumbled: 'I'm tired of all these old cliches. Go out and get me some new ones.' In this sense a case can be made for some of the older historical cliches. Perhaps students still need to be told that some grasp of Christian theology is, even more than Latin or German, or a diploma in Social Studies, a prerequisite for understanding the Reformation. They need to be reminded that the painful craft of writing decent English is still honourable, for it is even more now than when Philip Guedalla wrote that 'Historians' English is an industrial disease'. Likewise they need to be reminded that the English Reformation neither began nor ended at the White Cliffs of Dover.
(Ibid, pp.3-4)

1981

When one of the first Separatists attacked the Prayer Book responses for being 'like the tossing to and fro of tennis balls', he had in fact stumbled upon a true image, and the right kind of response is a phrase like 'And the same to you, mate,' and not the terrible 'And also with you'.
('Assessing the New Liturgies', in *Epworth Review*, September 1981, p.43)

The whole colour of 'our Liturgy' is affected by 'our hymns'. Those are what other churches have to listen to us about, where we really know, and there is the fount of an inspiration which touches the parts other communions cannot reach (by this medium). Bernard Manning very rightly said that a Church which let go of Watts and Wesley would have gone mad – and perhaps as a church we are heading for a nervous breakdown. He might have added a few more, such as Doddridge and the medieval hymns of J M Neale – it is the nineteenth-century ballast which should be jettisoned. By hard thought and prayer and taking a very great deal of care, our choice of hymns can really govern the whole mood and tone of our worship. With ditties like those of Sydney Carter, set to doleful tunes like that of the dismal Shakers' 'Lord of the Dance' (dance! have they never heard the Sailor's

Hornpipe or an Irish jig?) or the semi-literate effusions of Fred Kaan, it is quite another thing.
(Ibid, pp.44-5)

1982

Young men are never attracted by the call to mediocrity, and in every age rich young rulers have heard the call and not turned away from it – Benedict and Francis and Ignatius, and Thomas Newton, and assuredly John Wesley among them.
(*The Plant of Salvation*, a lecture given to the Friends of Wesley's Chapel)

Some years ago I wrote what I would not now retract, of John Wesley's evangelical Arminianism, that it was an 'Optimism of Grace'. In an age which had come to believe that salvation was only for the few, Wesley proclaimed what his brother sang: 'For all, for all my saviour died, For all my Lord was crucified.' But we have also to admit that under Whitefield and the Anglican evangelicals, and among the preachers in Wales and Scotland and America, it was Calvinist theology, a different theological package deal, which was as influential in converting men and women as 'our doctrines'.

And I do not think we quite solve the problem when we point out that both Arminianism and Calvinism were within the one embrace of our Augustinian view of man's sin and of sovereign, saving grace, that both preached fundamentally the same good news for sinners – and that, as Wesley says in one of the letters [to 'John Smith'], 'You have not to fight against notions, but against sin.' Shall we perhaps say that what mattered in the case of John Wesley was not 'our doctrines' so much as 'our discipline' – the fact that his view of holiness, so different from that of William Law in this respect, was social holiness, that he put at the heart of his movement the Christian cell, the *koinonia*, the sanctified and pardoned community, the communion of saints? It would be truer, I think, to say that was Wesley's share in the Evangelical Revival, that which became the 'People called Methodists' and in due season the Methodist Church, which arose from the combination of 'our doctrines' and 'our discipline', as the Minutes of the early conferences display perfectly; 'our doctrines' and 'our discipline' – together with 'our hymns' and 'our literature' form a coherent whole.

So 'our doctrines' are not a rigid pattern. They form a shape, but it is a flexible one – more like a cricket field with two slips and a gully or perhaps now and then a silly point and a long on – but all of them

113

guarding and pointing to what is more important than any of them, the divine saving action of God Himself in his dear Son, and through the operation of his Holy Spirit, pardoning and sanctifying his children by bringing them into such a communion with himself as must always grow and can never end: 'Changed from glory into glory'.
(Ibid)

1984

To those who have asked in recent weeks, 'What do you think Luther has to say to our world?' I have refused the question. He was not born into our world, and what he had to say to his world he said in about a hundred folio volumes. He thought he lived in the last days of history, in a world, to use a crude image, well into injury time and when the final whistle might blow at any moment.

It is we, the living, who are called to speak to our world and if we take words from the illustrious dead it is we who use them or manipulate them to underline our own views. What we take from the past, principles, examples, saws and instances, are law, not gospel. History is the dead book. The Word of God is alive.
(From a sermon preached in Westminster Abbey on the 500th anniversary of the birth of Martin Luther; *Epworth Review*, May 1984, p.42)

I do not know what share young people have had in the recent commemoration, but it is very important to understand that in its beginnings the Reformation captured the imagination and the hearts of the young, gave them something to sing about, something worth dying for. Luther's first hymn was a popular ballad, passed from hand to hand on a single sheet, about two young men, little more than boys, who were burned in the market place in Brussels for the Gospel's sake.
(Ibid, pp.42-3)

* * *

In default of ordained clergy who would share the costly dangers of his work [Wesley] created an order of preachers. They were not cut from the same cultural cloth as the regular clergy, but of a tougher, if coarser fabric. They were not officer class, but officer material. But then, the greatest need of Christ's Church Militant there in eighteenth century England was for such a glorious regiment of sergeant majors.
('John Wesley – the Man', in *The People Called Methodists*, p.8)

Are there then two Augustines – one Evangelical, the other Catholic? Henry Marou sees him as a kind of El Greco figure – and one remembers the anguished, ecstatic, beautiful Augustine of Bernini's in St Peter's, Rome. Whereas for Protestants he is a Rembrandt – in all the light and dark of his chiaroscuro. Perhaps we all need an *aggiornamento* before we can cure this double vision, and perhaps find in Augustine's *sola gratia* an end to dire division . . . For Augustine is the champion of grace which is the optic nerve of the Christian religion. It is he who binds it all together, individual salvation and the great *Totus Christus*, Christ in Head and Members. We have not done with him. He is the Halley's comet of Church History. We need to listen to him in a world whose sick and disintegrating culture is beginning more and more to resemble that crumbling world in which he died. If our theologians are not playing games, chucking stones at broken bottles on Dover Beach, then they must face the questions raised by him. An unremitting, agonizing search for faith, fighting one by one and exposing one by one impressive, pretentious, and in the end bogus world views, yet on which the world would always beat the Christians on a card vote. And the even more desperate enterprise of men's and women's hearts – bodies and souls out of gear, meaning and control in a world which has almost slipped beyond human control. And over and against it the fact of God, awful in his majesty, infinite in his compassion, who knows it all, and who has met our need in all its darkness and depth, shedding his love abroad and raising our hearts and minds to his eternal love. These are matters framed but not over-ridden by any world-view, whether of Ptolemy, or Copernicus, or Newton or Einstein, but which speaks to us in time from another kind of time, another dimension altogether. We have not done with Augustine. He will be back, in some new crisis of renewal, and when he comes to that new age, he will cheer humanity on, a day's march nearer home, the City of God.

('Augustine: Father of Both Reformations', a lecture delivered in Cambridge on 13 November 1985; in *Epworth Review*, May 1990, pp.79-80)

* * *

Perhaps I might repeat myself after thirty years . . . 'The Methodist tradition is not something which the antiquarians, church historians, theologians and romantics can recapture for us by ferreting among books and liturgies, or by re-thinking, re-stating, re-assessing Methodist doctrines. We cannot go back to Wesley, or to some reconstructed original Methodism. If we try, it will be with us as with those men who tried to find the invisible man by removing his clothes one by one until they took off the last layer, and with that made him completely disappear.

That way lies dilettantism and antiquarianism and the peril of making John Wesley into a ventriloquist's dummy, into whom we simply read our own opinions. Be warned by the sons of Gibeon in the book of Joshua. You remember how they dressed up in old garments, put old sacks upon their asses, old wineskins rotten and mended, provisions dry and mouldy, and said to the men of Israel, 'We have come from a far country. Make a covenant with us.' But God's people, who are not so easily conned or kidded as some people suppose, recognized them for Johnnies-come-lately from down the road. And so, when we have our proper discussions about stocks and stoles and scapulars and pectoral crosses (and perhaps it is an advantage that, from being blackbirds for two centuries, we now begin to look like budgerigars[25]), when we do these things, quite properly (and I dare say that it is all an improvement), let us remember that, to the great majority of our fellow countrymen we are just a lot of dropouts, walking along Dover Beach, from which the sea of faith has long since disappeared. Let us also remember Samuel Johnson's 'O let us not be found, when our Master calls, ripping the lace off our waistcoats, but the spirit of contention from our souls and tongues.'
(Jubilee Sermon, preached in Wesley's Chapel, London 2 November 1985; printed in the *Bulletin* of the Methodist Sacramental Fellowship, No.115, pp.5-6)

1986

Despite their claim to be the true Catholic remnant in England, the Non-Jurors could not but feel their isolation. Utterly opposed to Rome, detesting the Lutheran and Reformed Churches, counting the English Dissenters as little better than heathen men and publicans, the Non-Jurors found it difficult to give practical expression to their zeal for the unity of all Christians, so often declared, and like some modern

---

25 The editor of the MSF *Bulletin* commented that Rupp himself, 'resplendent in his doctrinal robes', looked 'more like a splendid macaw than a budgerigar'.

successors, made up for their lack of service towards their separated brethren at home, by compassing sea and land to love the brethren they had not seen.
(*Religion in England 1688-1791*, p.19)

Those who labour for the cause of Christian unity need the skills of horticulturists rather than those of engineers . . .
(Ibid, p.84)

It would be interesting to know how early the Church of England developed a social contempt for Nonconformity, perhaps the nastiest disability inflicted by the Establishment on its separated brethren.
(Ibid, p.167)

To these new currents [in science and philosophy] the Dissenting seminaries were more open, though perhaps more vulnerable to the spirit of the time. Hidebound Oxford and Cambridge might be, but there are times, as superficial fashions sweep along, when there is something to be said for having an extra skin.
(Ibid, p.177)

Rich men furnished with ability have always had a part to play in the history of the Church, though they have sometimes been an intolerable nuisance.
(Ibid, p.189)

Greatly over-simplifying, it might be said that in the sixteenth and seventeenth centuries the Christian Churches had lost control of two powerful traditions of the human spirit, one in letters, philosophy and science which we may roughly call humanism, and the other a tradition of social justice, of the rights and liberties of men. Both of these were now returning in confrontation with the Church, one-sided, anti-clerical, even atheistic, refracted and bent indeed, but to them by reason of its own failure, the Church could not reply with an unqualified 'No' while equally unable to give an unequivocal 'Yes'.
(Ibid, p.201)[26]

26 For a more extended treatment of this theme, see 'Doctrine of Man' in *The Expository Times*, Vol. 61, p.100

Perhaps we should be careful about the word 'conversion' which the eighteenth century did not use nearly as much as did the nineteenth century, and if we think that Sankey and Moody or Dr Billy Graham were saying and doing what Whitefield and Wesley were saying and doing we may run into serious misconceptions. The unending debate as to what really happened to John Wesley on 24 May 1738 has been blurred by reading back into it nineteenth-century ideas. Drastic it was, but I think John Wesley never talked of it as his 'conversion', and in fact what nineteenth-century Evangelicals described as one experience of 'conversion' was for the Methodists a complexity in which at least three of what they called 'our doctrines' – 'justification by faith, the new birth, and the witness of the Spirit – were all involved.
(Ibid, pp.326-7)

The solemnity of the Puritans and the sombreness of the Evangelicals can be exaggerated. There is more music and laughter in *Pilgrim's Progress* than in the writings of John Donne or William Law. Joy was a hallmark of the evangelical experience, and 'dour' the least apposite of all adjectives applied to Methodist spirituality.
(Ibid, p.451)

* * *

One of the great turning points in church history was when Saint Augustine entered into such a living dialogue with Saint Paul, and began a kind of nuclear reaction, which took in the Reformers Luther and Calvin, the Catholic Reformation and the Evangelical Revival, a dialogue the end of which is not yet.
(M.S.F. *Bulletin*, No. 115, p.6)

Catholic spirit? Where was it in the eighteenth century? Leaders of the Church of England, with incredible smugness and arrogance, dismissed one thousand years of rationality and spirituality. Bishop Stillingfleet dismissed the Lady Julian of Norwich as 'blasphemous tittle-tattle'. Archbishop Herring thought that all that mattered about Saint Anselm was that he was a traitor to his king. 'John Smith' (perhaps an archbishop) told Wesley that Saint Augustine was 'a flighty and injudicious author' and that Saint Bernard was 'enthusiastically inclined'. Bishop Lavington spoke to Wesley of 'those nasty, ridiculous, crackbrained, wicked saints – Saint Francis, Saint Dominic and Saint Ignatius'. But turn to John Wesley's Christian Library – fifty volumes of every century and every communion, touching the heights

118

and depths of grace itself, and you will say, 'There in the eighteenth century was catholicity. There was the catholic spirit.'
(Ibid, p.8)

Bunyan's happy band of pilgrims – not one of them, not a single one of them, in ecclesiastical dress, any more than were the first apostles. We have to guard the apostolate of the laity in our time. I have always said that what Methodism has to offer the ecumenical movement is not buildings or music or liturgies or theologies, but good Christian people, thousands and thousands of humble Christian men and women, and I hope that we shall remember them at a time when, if I mistake not, there is a rapidly widening gulf between the clerisy of our churches (the ministers and leading laymen) and the men and women, the people in the pew.
(Ibid, p.9)

As you ponder your role for the next half century, or rather, the tasks his wisdom has assigned to you, whether you think of yourselves as called to be a kind of Waffen SS of the Church, or, perhaps, a swashbuckling company of musketeers full of spirit and panache (Oh, that you were!), or as a mixture of pirates and policemen, we must in spirit put those things behind us today, and simply relax in the wonder of the gospel.
(Ibid, p.10)

* * *

There are many of the Psalms which strike notes which are silent on most of our English spiritual pianos, experiences of a depth of suffering which silence us and abash us in our comfortable homes.
(*Methodist Recorder*, May 29, 1986)

* * *

WHAT! NO MOUNT ZION?

The headline is not the caption of an early Chad cartoon, but the cry of Hopeful when he and Christian were met by Atheist, who came to them with his back turned on Mount Zion, and who fell about with laughter at the foolish delusions of men who believed in such a place.

Lately it has become an 'in' thing to talk about death: the Americans have invented 'Thanatology' and pastoral conferences spend time discussing how to prepare the dying and console the bereaved. But I suspect looking forward to heaven, with anything like joy, is not high on their agenda . . . Our religion nowadays has breadth, no question of that, but it has very little depth and has given up height in the sense of a hope which bids men look forward and upward, beyond history and across the frontiers of death . . . The makers of our new hymn book, faced with the sagging balloon of a Methodist spirituality rapidly losing height, cast overboard with all speed the ballast of some of the best hymns about heaven.

(*Methodist Recorder*, June 26, 1986)

ENVOY

Gordon Rupp's last paper, published posthumously, was, appropriately, about Luther's closing years:

In the last act of John Osborne's play *Martin Luther*, he brings Staupitz back to the Black Cloister in Wittenberg (he had in historical fact been dead for some years) simply to make him comment on the loneliness of what had once been the thronged life of the Augustinian monastery. 'It's so odd. The place was full of men. And now there's only you and Katy. It's very, very strange.' Strange indeed, and quite untrue. We know of one travelling scholar who was warned not to stay with the Luthers because their home was always crowded out. The house was full: unmarried and marriable spinsters, convalescents, derelict widows, refugee pastors, orphaned children, undergraduate boarders, ushers with their pupils, scholars, foreigners. It was a bustling Liberty Hall which often brought the mistress of the house to anger and near despair.[27] There were very few of those blessed moments when a husband and wife look at one another in the silence and sigh with relief that all their guests have gone! And not least from 1530 onwards there were scribes who wrote down his conversation, so that breakfast and dinner became mini-Rotary Club affairs. It was their memories which became the staple of Henry Bell's Table Talk. When James Boswell in one of his sublimely silly moments sprawled all over the tomb of Melanchthon in Wittenberg to write a 'Wish you were here' note to Samuel Johnson, he never mentioned Luther, whom he thought Johnson would dislike. But in fact 'Luther and Samuel Johnson' would make a very profitable article. Both were sages, worth listening to, worth recording, though Luther's utterances have unhappily been deprived of that 'Sitz im Leben' which is half the fun in Boswell.

Their friends tended to show them off, at worst as though they were performing bears. Each could be horribly rude, each could be generous, wise, and full of pawky humour, so offensive to the pious ease of the Rev Obadiah Sedgewick and the Westminster Fathers . . .

And in the background was Kate Luther, one of his better sparring partners. She was the manager, and kept him from giving everything away. For he had no venality in him and died poorer than Erasmus. Others made fortunes from his books and bibles, but he got nothing and

---

27 Cf *The Righteousness of God*, p.6: 'We know how it irked Frau Luther to play Martha to half a dozen male Marys who made Luther talk while the food got cold.'

at the end of his life was grateful for a small pension from the King of Denmark. He bought one or two small properties, but the biggest deal was when his wife was able to buy her brother's farm at Zuladorf with a few cattle and pigs. 'Luther and Pigs' is an interesting minor theme, for they had for him some of the affectionate fascination of Lord Emsworth for the Empress of Blandings.

Like many elderly people he thought the world was getting worse, the seasons were more inclement, and trees not so long lived. The older historians talked about 'Weltpessimismus', but today we might call Luther a Doomwatcher, contemplating the sins of men, of which the decay in manners and morals, and the growing violence, were true signs of the end of time.

('The Old Man Luther', in *Faith, Heritage and Witness*, 1987, pp.27-8)

Once this old man had shaken nations and moved the great ones of the earth. Now history passed on, its surface hardly ruffled. Five hundred years later men came to that little town, where he had been born and where he died, to do him honour. They included a Cardinal and Archbishops, and representatives of that great world-wide communion of his sons in the gospel. Had he chosen a text it might have been, 'Give God the glory. As for this man we know that he is a sinner.' For, as his last written words seem to have said, 'Poor beggars aren't we all, and that's the truth.' Yet he might have been pleased to know that after 500 years so many would still thank God for his servant, Martin Luther.

(Ibid, p.33)

INDEX

laity, 94, 119
    priesthood of all believers, 11,
       47 *see also* priesthood
language, 11, 62, 68, 91, 94, 99,
    105, 106, 110, 112
Lidgett, John Scott, 47
Luther, Martin: 13, 45, 55(2),
    58, 81, 96, 103, 114
    family background, 50-1
    and Hitler, 13-14
    and Dr Johnson, 23-4
    Lectures on Hebrews, 64-5
    old age, 121-2
    Osborne on, 64, 121
    prayer, 97
    Word and Spirit, 34

Marxism, 28, 69, 96
    see also Communism
media, 85, 102
medieval Church, 11, 98-9
Methodism, 24-25, 26, 89, 115-6
    doctrines, 113-14, 118
    early itinerants, 12, 114
    radicals, 90
    Sacrament, 18
    Wesleyanism, 20
ministerial training, 32-3, 75
Moravianism, 79
Muntzer, Thomas, 46-7, 82-3,
    97-8, 101
mysticism, 80, 109

New Testament scholarship, 88
Newman, John Henry, 81-2, 110
Non-Jurors, 116-17
Nonconformity, 38, 59-60, 66;
nonconformist conscience, 21, 39

original sin, 45
    total depravity, 70

Paul, St, 19
persecution, 18

Pilgrim's Progress, 37, 118, 119,
    120
politics, 20-1
prayer, 91, 97
preaching, 72, 104, 110
priesthood, 67 *see also* laity
prophecy, 34-6, 38
Protestantism, 24, 25, 26(2), 59,
    96 *see also* Reformation
Psalms, 23, 53-4, 90, 91, 93, 98,
    119
Puritanism, 11, 18, 25, 38-9, 42,
    48, 57, 66, 100, 110, 118

Reformation, the, 14-15, 16, 17,
    24, 34, 59, 61, 82, 87, 88-9.
    see also Protestantism
Restoration period, 65, 67
resurrection of the body, 71-2
Roman Catholicism, 27, 86-7

Sabbatarianism, 96
salvation, plan of, 29
satire, 99, 109
Scholasticism, 79
secularism, 47-8, 59.
    see also humanism
social justice, 27, 31, 68-9, 117
sociology, 72, 94

theology/doctrine, 22, 29, 40,
    41-2, 81, 87, 103-4, 106, 112,
    113
truth, 12, 30, 80

Utopianism, 30

Wesley, John, 12, 26, 42, 68,
    78-9, 106, 113, 118
wonder, 70
World Council of Churches, 103
World Methodism, 43, 77
worship, 104-5, 112-13